Sick City

Disease, Race, Inequality and Urban Land

Patrick M. Condon

Published by the James Taylor Chair at the University of British Columbia School of Architecture and Landscape Architecture.
Second Edition

Printed by Off the Common Books, Amherst MA.

Manufactured in the United States of America
10 9 8 7 6 5 4 3 2 1

Keywords: pandemic, racism, America, housing, land price, land rent, sprawl, inequality, wage gap, cities, suburbs, crowding, US Constitution, planning policy, zoning, inclusive zoning, cash in lieu, Cambridge, Portland, Henry George, Vienna housing.

ISBN : 978-1-7774560-0-9

Contents

Resource web site with color illustrations, web links, and free e-book

https://justicelandandthecity.blogspot.com/

Acknowledgments

After writing more than a few acknowledgments, I know that very few people read them. So for you dear reader a few surprises: this is not your usual acknowledgment.

I want to acknowledge my uncle Larry Cashin who gave me my start in this business when he hired a long haired college dropout in 1972 and sent me out into a poor neighborhood in my home town of Brockton Mass. My job was to save adolescents from a life of crime and incarceration. I am not sure how much good I did, but I am sure his biggest success was me.

I also want to acknowledge my sister Margie who I believe is my only sibling to read all of my books cover to cover. Rest in peace Margie.

Of course my kids deserve a mention: to Alanna, Ryan, Kate and Will. You will never know how proud I am of you, and that marrying your moms was, in retrospect, the best two things I ever did!

And now a nod to all the politicians of the world. It takes a lot of guts to stand for election. I saw that in my own family. It can take a toll. Thanks dad. Among these I even number the infuriating Donald Trump, without whom this book would surely not have been written. A feeling of impotence married to unquenchable rage is a powerful motivator.

Then there are all the crazy Brown University graduates who descended on my home town in 1972 to save it from itself, never realizing that cities don't like to be saved. God love you all. You know who you are.

As for the academic side of things, thanks goes to the Lincoln Institute of Land Policy where I was exposed to the legacy of Henry George during my fellowship there. Then of course there are all the students I have shared time with for over three decades. It's still amazing to me that I got paid to do this job – I have the best job on the planet. Special thanks to former student and Master of Urban Design graduate Kaenat Seth who worked with me after graduation, helping with the research and production of this book.

Last but not least, thanks to all of my Canadian friends who put up with yet another know-it-all American in their midst. You may be right. You may live in the best country on the planet after all.

Dedication

I am sure that my other three kids will forgive me for dedicating this book to my eldest, Alanna Mallon. This is because she had the courage to put herself out there for election to council in the "People's Republic of Cambridge" Massachusetts, and because her struggles there informed this book.

Cambridge is a very very tough electorate to please. But you did, and won. Not only that, but when you faced re-election two years later, against the terrifying head winds blowing from the politically dominant left leaning Cambridge homeowners – homeowners who were all for saving the planet but not much for opening up their neighborhoods for affordable housing - you did the right thing. You accepted the possibility/probability of a humiliating defeat, lobbied hard for change, and you won. Not just that; but you also saw passed the country's most important affordable housing policy. It is now the model for other municipalities seeking to solve the housing crisis.

I (and your grandfather) could not be more proud of City of Cambridge Vice Mayor Alanna Mallon.

Preface to Canadian edition.

Sick City was written, as will become obvious, for an American audience. However, with the exception of the lasting influence of slavery on current US conditions, the problems discussed herein are much the same if not worse in Canada as in the US.

Major Canadian metropolitan areas, notably Toronto and Vancouver, are burdened with housing costs that are substantially higher than their American counterparts. By some measures the gap between wages and housing costs in Vancouver are the highest in the world. Why? Because urban land in Canada has become the most lucrative and safest investment asset to own in a world hungry for assets of all kinds.

Central banks in Canada, like central banks throughout the developed world are furiously printing money and keeping interest rates low to prevent the collapse of a market that underpins national financial "stability". It is a stability purchased at a huge cost, and largely on the backs of younger workers now absolutely priced out of the housing market and burdened by unaffordable rents.

As a result, younger workers and marginalized communities are now much more likely to suffer the effects of pandemic: through higher levels of employment in so called "front line" service industries where remote working is impossible; through being confined to more crowded apartments than is healthy; and through enduring long commutes forced by lack of affordable housing near jobs rich centres.

The argument, then, of this book is that by providing affordable housing more evenly throughout our metropolitan regions, these linked pathologies can be dramatically mitigated, and that we have the policy tools and the wealth necessary to succeed - should we have the heart and the determination to use them.

Preface

When, in the winter of 2020, the pandemic struck, I had just released a book named *Five Rules for Tomorrow's Cities*. In that book none of the following words can be found: disease, plague, pandemic, communicability or virus. So much for my skills with a crystal ball.

Then all my classes went on line.

Then the lockdown.

Faced with nothing but time to sit on my couch, and as frustrated and despondent as the rest of the world, I decided to write another book right away. And even though my academic career was largely focused in Canada, this book would be entirely focused on the USA, where I am from.

Prior to this time I was sure that at the age of 70 I was done with writing books. That *Five Rules* was my last kick at the can, so to speak. Well, the pandemic intervened. Very soon it became clear to me that the pandemic was making the inequalities of the American political economy all the more glaring, and that my 40 years of exploring how urban design intersected with ecological, social, and economic sustainability equipped me with certain possibly useful ways of looking at the problem, and the time on my hands to do something about it.

But writing this kind of book takes a lot of time. It's usual for academics to take five years or so between books. Since the pandemic was an urgent matter and since, as I said, I had time on my hands, I resolved to write this book in months rather than years. And that's what I did.

Also, working with publishers of academic volumes consumes time no matter how fast you write, usually requiring a year or so for production. Life is too short (mine anyway) and this issue is too urgent. So this time I am taking a different approach. In the perhaps foolish notion that, now that we are all in a post COVID reality, a book like this one might do a bit of good, I want to get it into as many hands as possible as quickly as possible. Thus this book is being distributed for free in the electronic version and sold at cost in the physical version. What this process sacrifices by not getting this book into bookstores and university libraries (heck, I have tenure, what do I care) it makes up for (I hope) by letting this book be freely copied and distributed without copyright issues getting in the way.

Naturally, as its author, I think that the contents are important. It would be foolish of me to presume the reader will necessarily agree; but if you do please cast the bread of this book upon the waters.

- Patrick Michael Condon, of Brockton, Massachusetts, USA

Introduction

America is confronted with a host of overlapping crises. The current pandemic, systemic racism, economic inequality and housing affordability are all at a critical stage. It is the hypothesis of this volume that urban land, its location, ownership, price, and the sacrifices people have to make to gain access to it, is a large part of the problem and can be a large part of the cure for these overlapping crises. And to avoid confusion, in the volume when we refer to "urban land" we mean both land in traditional "center cities" and land in the so-called suburbs where the majority of American urban residents reside. Eighty percent of Americans now live in urban areas, struggling to find decent homes on land that, while covering only 5 percent of the surface area of the country, accounts for over 80 percent of its real-estate dollar value.

The problems taken up herein do not lack for attention by the media, academics and citizens. Racial and economic inequality, stagnant wages, unaffordable housing and, most recently, global pandemics are exhaustively covered (albeit with precious few solutions to point to). Hardly mentioned is how these nested issues all, in the end, come down to urban land. Urban land prices have inflated so much that the cost of rent and home purchases has risen out of reach of average wage earners. Black families, barred for a century or more from gaining access to land, now control a tiny fraction of the wealth held by the average White family. Poorly paid front-line workers fighting the current pandemic (think orderlies, and grocery clerks – now called "essential") cannot live close to work, endangering them through long commutes and exposed workplaces. Immigrant families crowd a dozen people into overpriced rental units, spreading disease both in their homes and in their neighborhoods.

What distinguishes this volume from other works on these topics is the contention that it is the land under the building, and its price, that is far more important than any other single factor in determining who gets sick, who struggles to keep a roof over their heads, and who lives paycheck to paycheck. Or stated another way, our problems are caused by the

Diverging income inequality trajectories

Source: WID.world (2017). See wir2018.wid.world for data series and notes.

In 2016, 12% of national income was received by the top 1% in Western Europe, compared to 20% in the United States. In 1980, 10% of national income was received by the top 1% in Western Europe, compared to 11% in the United States.

Figure 0-1. Trends in American income share since 1980. Trends in income share and share of wealth are different. Trends in wealth inequality are far more extreme. Illustration based on data from World Inequality Database WID.world.

hyper-financialization of urban land.[1] By this, we mean the decades-long shift from a housing market that once struck a rough balance between local housing costs and average metropolitan area wages, to one where this link is broken. Real estate is now largely priced, not for its value as housing, but for its value as an asset in a global marketplace hungry for assets of any kind. Urban land is now traded and valued just like stocks and bonds (if you doubt this, explore the explosive growth of

---

1   For an accessible and riveting look at how housing is now an asset class, see the film PUSH accessible here: http://www.pushthefilm.com/

real-estate-investment trust[2] [REITs] hedge funds) and is similarly subject to simultaneous shifts in real-estate prices on both sides of the globe. Rents are unaffordable not because landlords are greedy but because the land under the apartment building has tripled in price in many locations. Mortgages are increasingly out of reach, not because it's so much more expensive to build a home, but because the cost of a suburban home is now governed by the price of the dirt below it.

In this volume, we use the words land "rent" and "price" interchangeably. This is in keeping with how economists use the term rent when they refer to land value. Land "price" is generally thought of as 15-20 years' worth of "rent" needed to "amortize" the same land. For reasons explained later in this volume, and to distinguish the commonplace meaning of rent (say the monthly payment for an apartment for example) from the way that economists use the term, the word Rent, when used in this second technical sense, will be capitalized.

The current problem – the pandemic.

City dwellers of color, recent immigrants, and the poor more generally have been hit hardest by the 2020 pandemic. Many media voices have speculated that urban density is the cause for this disparity, or personal hygiene, or crowded buses. In contrast, in this volume, you will find evidence that inequitable exposure to disease results from the way land is priced and distributed. Land costs, and thus home costs, are now substantially out of balance with wages, an imbalance that has been gradually widening since the 1970s when average home prices were only 4 times average annual gross wages. Now the difference is 12 times annual wages.

Rising urban land costs don't just affect home purchase prices, they also affect the value of land under rental buildings and thus, over time, inflate rents. As a consequence, immigrant families are forced to crowd a dozen people into apartments suitable for four, creating a rich environment for the transfer of disease.

We have stalled raising the minimum wage for decades, to the point where full-time service workers, those closest to the "front line" against COVID-19, earn poverty-level incomes – low-wages that are largely devoted to paying landlords.

We have, for centuries, denied African-Americans access to their

---

2   REITs went from zero in assets in 1960 when they were first legalized to their current value of over 3 trillion dollars USD (Nareit n.d.)

share of the land necessary to build wealth, real-estate wealth that for American Whites has been the principal pathway to financial security.

We have divided metropolitan regions on a vast scale by race and class, Balkanizing urban land to the detriment of sustainable social and economic function.

We have concentrated job sites far distant from affordable homes, forcing unnecessarily long daily worker migrations on steroidal highways and dangerously crowded transit systems.

Disease and race

Despite substantial gains in education, Black Americans have no more personal wealth now than in 1950.[3] The small gains in wealth made by Black Americans during the 1980s and 1990s were wiped out by the Great Recession of 2008. Black Americans are almost as likely to live in segregated areas now as in the 1970s;[4] are far more likely to hold front-line service jobs[5] (grocery clerk, delivery driver, orderly, bus driver, etc.) than American Whites. They are the recipients of a police presence that at times feels like a military occupation and experience a deficit of the good schools and civic infrastructure that White suburban dwellers enjoy. These factors combine to ensure that American Blacks will, on average, be less likely to work from home, less able to stay home from work, and will be in far greater daily contact with other endangered and endangering people than their counterparts. All this a full 50 years after Congress passed fair housing, voting rights, and anti-discrimination legislation. As explored in Chapter one, these factors combine to make Black Americans up to four times more likely to die of COVID-19 than Whites. On average, their daily routine moves them from homes they don't own and can hardly afford, to transit systems with poor ventilation, to jobs where they share air space with other similarly endangered people every day. Why is this so? The commonplace answer is that systemic racism explains these income and wealth gaps. Less acknowledged (and in many ways easier to correct) is that the invisible hand of urban land prices shifts marginalized groups into dangerous and unequal living circumstances. While the pathology of racism – our American original sin – is now, yet again, proving itself tremendously difficult to cure, policy tools

---

3   (Brooks, 2020)
4   (The Economist, 2018)
5   (Salsberg, 2018)

are readily available to cure the problem of urban land price inflation, should we simply choose to use them.

Disease and inequality broadly

The travails of Black Americans are not theirs alone. Increasingly, a younger generation of White Americans is experiencing similar stresses and dangers. The pandemic is also exposing how racial classes that in previous generations may have experienced privilege, are no longer quite so blessed. An even larger wave of inequality is sweeping up previously protected economic classes and age cohorts.

The words that Martin Luther King wrote a half-century ago about the ways that the Black revolution revealed even larger injustices also seems to apply to the pandemic:

> *"The Black revolution is much more than a struggle for the rights of Negroes... It is forcing America to face all its interrelated flaws — racism, poverty, militarism and materialism. It is exposing evils that are rooted deeply in the whole structure of our society. It reveals systemic rather than superficial flaws and suggests that radical re-construction of society itself is the real issue to be faced."* [6]

Similarly, the pandemic is also revealing a whole new layer of the American underclass: college-educated Millennials barred from access to the wealth that their parents enjoyed, serving in low-wage, precarious "McJobs" or the gig economy, with burdensome school loans to pay off and no reasonable hope of owning a home or achieving retirement security. All while America completes its shift from an industrial economy to an economy based on the same service categories that are currently endangering Blacks and immigrants. Why? Because neoliberal economics[7], with its global free flow of capital and the associated worldwide erosion of equitable taxation has led the country to a state where 400 Americans now have more combined wealth than the entire UK, and where the

---

6   (King, Martin Luther. May 10, 1967, Speech to The Hungry Club Forum, Atlanta Georgia. https://www. theatlantic.com/magazine/archive/2018/02/martin-luther-king-hungry-club-forum/552533/)

7   (Smith n.d.) There is no avoiding the use of this term from economics. In this volume, neoliberalism is used to signify a philosophy of political economy that favors a reduced role for the state and an increased role for private enterprise. It gained political currency in the 1980s when embraced by Margaret Thatcher and Ronald Reagan. It is called "neoliberalism" because it revives principles of laissez-faire free-market economic thinking from the original "liberal" period of the 18th century. For the purposes of this volume, neoliberalism and liberalism are largely the same but for a key difference in how they treat the value of land. This difference is discussed in Chapter two.

share of national income of the bottom 50 percent of Americans crashed from 20 percent in 1980 of all income to 13 percent now. During those same four decades, the share of income claimed by the top one percent of earners doubled from 10 percent of the total to over 20 percent.

Disease and housing

This shift in wealth and income might not have been so hard to accept if it were not accompanied by large increases in the cost of housing, increases that were double the rate of inflation. As total wealth flowed in ever-increasing amounts into the pockets of those who already had wealth, not just in the USA but worldwide (fueled by decades of historically low interest rates and the corollary: a glut of money in the hands of the investor class), the value of all asset classes has skyrocketed. This "everything bubble"[8] is nice if you are rich and the value of your investments grow and grow. It's not so great when you are living paycheck to paycheck like almost half of Americans,[9] and the cost of housing gets bid up higher and higher by the insatiable appetites of the investor class.

The value[10] of urban land now nearly matches the total market capitalization of every corporation in the US,[11] and as that value inflates, the gap between wage-earner incomes and the cost of a home or rent continues to widen. The result is an unhealthy crowding in the homes of immigrants, people of color, and the wage-earning class generally, a crowding not seen since the 1930s. The data now clearly shows that it is not residential density that is the vector for disease – i.e. the number of units per acre – but the number of people per square foot in the housing units themselves. Disease passes in shared kitchens and bathrooms, not in the elevators and lobbies of expensive high-rises.

Disease and urban design

The disease vector of crowded apartments is echoed in the inequitable

---

8   The "everything bubble" refers to our current global financial circumstances, where national banks intervene in markets to prop up asset values should they start to decline. This, of course, influences the price of land, making it a sounder investment - and thus more likely to attract free capital - than it would be otherwise. (Summers, 2017)
9   Forty three percent of Americans are "poor" or "low-income" according to the Institute for Policy Studies report (Sarkar, 2018) (Barber, 2018), which means either they are grindingly poor or are just scraping along and unable to buy a home or acquire other forms of wealth. As a result, 40 percent of Americans cannot come up with $400 should they need to respond to an emergency. (Youn, 2019)
10   (Loyd, 2019)
11   It is likely that the value of US urban land actually exceeds the capital value of American corporations because much of the capital value of corporations is tied up in the land they own. That's not to mention the many corporations whose entire enterprise is the management of urban property.

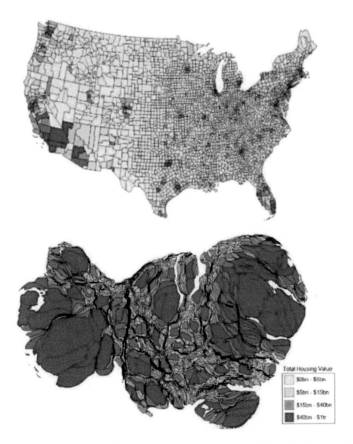

Figure 0-2. The concentration of housing value by location (top view) disguises the overwhelming land wealth in urban areas. The concentration of housing value is revealed in its actual dollar values (bottom view) showing how dramatically urban land outprices rural land in America. Illustration by Metrocosm, based on data from US Census and Lincoln Institute of Land Policy

layout of our metropolitan regions. American metropolitan regions have, over the past seven decades, become ever more separated by income and race. Auto-mobility and the supporting infrastructure of limited-access freeways have enabled an urban landscape where income classes and ethnic groups are typically separated by scores of miles. In consequence, low-income and minority enclaves have become ever more confined. In these neighborhoods of concentrated disadvantage, the crowding mentioned above is exacerbated by the presence of similarly disadvantaged residents on the streets and in the cafés, dramatically increasing the chances that the person next to you in the coffee shop is infected compared to those sitting in a similar café in exclusive areas. National housing policy[12] conspires to make this worse, focusing already parsimonious housing funds in already poor neighborhoods, missing an opportunity to dilute the disease-concentrating effects of race and class segregation.

Disease and transport

American transportation and land-use policy also contribute to this crisis. We have tolerated dysfunctional regional planning regimes where separate small municipalities within a Balkanized metropolitan region have virtual veto power over what kinds of jobs can locate within them and what income classes can live there. The net result is, compared to other advanced economies, American workers are forced to travel longer distances from the housing they can best afford to the jobs for which they can best compete.[13] This pattern ensures that low-paid service workers, whether they commute by car or transit, are likely to carry infection from their disadvantaged homes and neighborhoods to the grocery stores and hairdressers of the leafy suburbs where they are employed. Much attention has been focused on transit as a probable vector for infection, but a more careful analysis of the data reveals that it is inequality that moves the plague, either by car or by transit or by both.

Injustice and the city

In short, it is in the very pattern and design of American metropolitan regions that we find a picture of inequality and the pathways for disease. It is almost as if drawn with malicious intent. Using this lens to view the problem, we might see that the visitation of this plague, and our unique inability to control it, is built into the very DNA of the American city.

The issue of asset wealth in real estate

What can be done about all this? Certainly ungluing the pieces of the urban puzzle and arranging them more equitably will take time. We might begin by recognizing that the metropolitan city is essentially the land

---

12   (Berg, 2014) (Thrush, 2020)
13   The US has the longest average commuting distance of any advanced nation except Austria, where most commuters either walk, bike or take the train. In Vienna, that's 67 percent . In the US, the walk, bike, transit share ranges from a vanishingly small 2 percent in Indianapolis to a "high" of 40 percent in New York. San Francisco is second with 27 percent. Most American metropolitan areas have a bike, walk, transit share of between 5 and 10 percent. (Wikipedia, 2020)

within its borders, the buildings placed upon that land and the pattern of how those buildings are distributed. Key to understanding the problem of this moment is to understand the importance of urban land itself – literally the dirt under buildings – and how much that dirt costs. What actually governs our city design is not really within the power of developers or planners, but almost entirely a function of how much urban dirt costs in any particular location. Using this lens, we might see that increasing inequality is reflected in how disadvantaged Americans (and in this we include the 40 percent of Americans living paycheck to paycheck) have less and less access to the land they need. The invisible hand of land economics overwhelms any rational government response to a degree almost unknown in other developed nations. Indeed, it reveals how the efforts of both entrepreneurs and wage earners eventually enrich not primarily the workers or the owners themselves, but are absorbed into the price of urban land. One hundred entrepreneurs who enrich a district with an attractive variety of shops and services will soon be rewarded with rent increases (and associated land value increases) that threaten their survival. Thus the benefits of their efforts accrue passively to those who own the land below their shops. As this process plays out region-wide, the pressure of land value increase rises to the point where the economy strains under the weight of housing inequality for wage earners while entrepreneurs are robbed of their gains.

Georgist thinking

This insight described above is not new. Henry George,[14] the American autodidact economist became famous[15] [16] in the late 19th-century for clearly describing how the efforts of both entrepreneurs and workers got sucked into the cost (Rent) of urban land to the detriment of both classes. His work was attacked by neoclassical economists, financed by gilded-era railroad/land barons,[17] who argued that land was not passive, but a productive class of capital akin to a factory. Sadly, the railroad barons held sway[18] and we are now the victims of their success. We will return to

---

14   (Gafney, 1994)
15   (De Mille, 1993)
16   (George, 1900)
17   (Gafney, 1994) Neoclassical economics is similar to neoliberal economics and the terms are often used interchangeably. Both are free-market and limited-government economic theories. Neoclassical is earlier, reviving classical economic theories of the 18th century in the 19th. Neoliberal comes later in the mid-20th. The simplest way to distinguish them is to remember that neoclassical theory mostly concerns questions of microeconomics, while neoliberal theory concerns questions of macroeconomics.
18   (Ibid.)

this topic later in this volume; but for now, this acknowledgment of the historical durability of this debate will suffice.

Figure 0-3. Henry George. Image: Wikimedia Commons.

Racial exclusion from American wealth is primarily exclusion from land

For American Blacks, centuries of racist practice and the resultant barriers to acquiring land are deeply baked into the system of land Rent. When slavery was finally abolished, many abolitionists argued for breaking up the vast plantations and dolling out family-sized acreage to the African-Americans who previously worked the land, as justified reparations for 200-plus years of slavery. Lincoln's plan to redistribute plantation land was thwarted by his assassination. His successor Andrew Johnson, a southern Democrat, canceled those plans.[19] Thus, plantation land stayed in the hands of White owners who then employed former slaves at wages

---

19   (Williams, 2010)

not much higher than the former cost of their "upkeep." This penurious system was reinforced by vagrancy laws[20] making it a crime to be without work, a crime punished by prison terms. These same prisoners were then forced into peonage to perform plantation labor no less arduous than their former slavery.

Absent any opportunity to build wealth in the form of farmland (and its associated farm infrastructure), African-Americans had little option but to travel north to rapidly expanding industrial cities. A very few were able to acquire sufficient wealth to establish an embryonic Black middle class, while the majority had to settle for whatever low-wage occupations (those not blocked by the objections of White union members) were available.[21] By the end of World War II, Blacks in both the rural south and northern urban ghettos had missed out on almost a century of opportunity to build the same wealth as their White peers. This handicap endures to this day. The halting progress made by African-Americans in joining the middle class through the same means as Whites, i.e. home ownership, was reversed by the 2008 Great Recession.[22] When property values crashed, predatory sub-prime loans trapped many people of color in non-renewable loans. Massive defaults among minority home purchasers was the result. Now the large majority of real-estate wealth is in the hands of White Americans.[23]

Millennial exclusion from capital

Younger American Whites now find themselves facing similar financial stresses as their African-American peers. Millennial-generation Whites are now also virtually closed out of the opportunity to build the wealth enjoyed by many of their parents (again, mostly in the form of home ownership). American wages for essentially all classes of workers have stayed flat (adjusted for inflation), with wages of hourly workers declining, while the cost of health care, education and especially housing has more than doubled (in real terms).[24] A near-zero interest rate environment has meant that the savings strategy of former generations, whereby saved money would compound with interest, while home prices stayed more or less flat, no longer works. In some cities, Boston for example,

---

20   (Tartar, n.d.)
21   (Crain, 2019)
22   (Mcintosh, 2020)
23   (Moore, 2016)
24   (Sarkar, 2018)

today's average wage earner, would need 22 years to save enough money for a 20 percent down payment on a decent home. For Baby Boomers, it took only five. [25]

What

The problem of both racial and income inequality, an inequality that in large part explains our national failure to manage the plague, is most manifest in unequal access to housing. Under contemporary economics, it's not flat-screen TVs that cost too much, it's not double-shot cappuccino or avocado toast that costs too much, it's housing. Furthermore, it's not the building itself that costs too much, it's the land under it. The cost per square foot of built space has not been the driver for the doubling and tripling of housing costs during this generation. A built square foot costs roughly the same as it did 30 years ago (adjusted for inflation).[26] It is, as Henry George pointed out, the land under the buildings that is the problem, and the international speculative inflation of urban land prices, driven by the "everything bubble," that we must somehow attack.

Where and who

The shape of our public infrastructure and the pattern of regional land uses that are served by it are decided by public policy. These decisions both respond to land value and determine land value. Sadly, all of these decisions typically benefit not the public at large, but the lucky owners of advantageously located land. Thus, the smartest people in the development game are the land speculators, men and women who make a handy living out of hunting up land that might be soon "improved" by the provision of a new highway, a new transit station, or a change in allowable land use. It seems shocking that our system of urban development pours trillions into the pockets of land speculators who effectively game this system while clawing back only a tiny portion, if any, of this new publicly created land value in the form of taxes. It was this outrageous inequity that led Henry George to dedicate his short life to advancing the case for a very high tax on land, with a commensurately lower tax on capital (like factories) and labor (wages). We currently hardly tax the riches poured into the pockets of land speculators. Citizens who need housing are the

25   (Olick, 2018)
26   The cost of building construction has increased, in the US and Canada, at just over the rate of inflation for a decade (with some variation city to city) (Canada, 2020)

injured party. Some American cities are trying to fix this failure. In this text we present these cases, and suggest politically viable expansions to these fledgling efforts.

What about the planet?

The above rightfully begs the question: How does all this tie into the climate change crisis? Illustrations of how the urban pattern of inequality

Figure 0-4. Intersection of two limited access freeways in Kansas City. Land owners benefited from new infrastructure expenditures in previously rural areas. Image: Google maps.

and poor health is also the urban pattern that contributes to ecological damage are taken up in Chapter three. The socially, racially, and clinically dysfunctional urban landscape described above also correlates with an urban landscape that requires unnecessarily high levels of polluting energy to power, while emptying the pockets of already severely stressed middle-class taxpayers to repair. In short, land cost drives urban form, which then drives climate change in ways not generally recognized.

Can it be fixed?

Yes. The good news is that a crisis can galvanize action like nothing else.

American precedents for change seem largely to appear, not in times of ease, but in times of deep societal pain. Slavery ended in the conflagration of the civil war. A global depression spawned a dramatic political reversal called the New Deal. The threat to America posed by global fascism reversed a century of "America First" politics. We argue that one can already see the building waves of resistance to injustice and inequality precipitated by the plague. Time will certainly tell, but all the indications of systemic change are clearly visible in our streets, in our neighborhoods, in Washington D.C. and in our hospitals. But this point is key, and will be argued in various ways in this volume: To attack the systemic dysfunctions in health, housing, land use and transportation, dysfunctions that are one of the root causes of racial and economic inequality, we must recognize that the cost of urban land (Rent) is not the consequence of benign forces of supply and demand, but a highly destructive form of monopoly. Just as monopoly practices by corporations demand legal limits, excessive land Rents do, too.

While it is not wise to understate the political, legal, and financial difficulties associated with shifting a system with such built-in inertia, many changes are already unfolding in American land-use policy that illuminates a path toward viable consensus-based solutions. It is the purpose of this volume to contribute to an emerging understanding of the influence of land Rents on our critical social and epidemiological pathologies – they are a consequence of the inequitable geographies of the American urban landscape, which are themselves driven by the damaging influence of land Rent.

The argument made herein, in sufficient detail to equip the reader with an understanding of an intentionally obscured aspect of otherwise dry real-estate economics, revives Progressive Era insights of Henry George and others; to wit: that privately held and traded urban land, due to its locational monopoly, drains all surplus value both from the efforts of wage earners and the entrepreneurial skills of their employers. Land Rents leave very little for them to share, while consigning regional economies to a state of perpetual precarity. "Surplus value" is not used here in the Marxist sense of a value rightfully belonging to workers but stolen by owners; but rather in the sense of Ricardo's "Law of Rents", which holds that Rents are set in such a way as to capture every cent of value that a location provides over free land distant from city centers. This problem is now being addressed, in as-yet halting and insufficiently scaled efforts, by municipalities using zoning and development taxing tools to influence land markets and provide permanently affordable workforce housing. Discussions of replicable solutions now gaining favor are in Chapters six and seven.

Conclusion

One hopes that this moment provides the required shock to the system necessary to shore up our crumbling defenses. Precedents exist: The New Deal, the fight against fascism, the walk on the moon. But in many ways this crisis seems different. In this crisis, all the festering sores of American culture, bandaged over for decades, have erupted – all too visible boils on the body politic. For reasons that are expanded on in the Chapters that follow, we argue that urban land is the hidden driver for many of these health, social and economic pathologies. At the time of this writing, presidential candidate Joseph Biden has adopted the campaign slogan "Build Back Better." Would that he succeeds. This volume attempts to illuminate how building back better can best succeed in the terms implied by this slogan if the problem caused by out-of-control land Rents is bravely faced.

In the following Chapters we will elaborate on the arguments incompletely made in this introduction. The focus remains on urban land and its connection to issues of equity and health. This topic was once on the top of our national agenda but has been suppressed in the discourse. Boiling all of these nested problems down to the singular problem of urban land is no longer commonplace in the debate. It should be. We provide evidence in support of this contention, trusting that this evidence will enhance our national deliberations.

Chapter 1

The pandemic and the city

Introduction

The question of city design and disease transmission is now a hot topic. The definition of design used in this volume is broad. City design is the aggregate consequence of both the physical features and arrangement of a city's buildings, and the transportation systems that support them. The focus is on how land use and transportation either exacerbate or mitigate systemic racism, health hazards, and economic inequality.

The average American who tries to understand how transmissible diseases spread is either overwhelmed by a deluge of contradictory information, or is driven by innate prejudices not informed by research. Neither case is healthy nor useful. The goal of this Chapter is to show that inequality is the vector for disease. The second goal of this Chapter is to show that disease, racial injustice and economic inequality are made worse by how we organize and assign urban land.

Race, inequality, the city and disease

The role of race as a factor in disease has assumed new importance. Data clearly indicates that Black and Brown Americans are three times more likely to become infected with COVID-19 than Whites,[27] — and we want to know why. It turns out that a century of systemic discrimination is the likely cause, manifest both in the economic geography of American cities and in the patterns of everyday life common to disadvantaged communities. These troubling urban economic geographies are not exclusive to minority populations, but minority communities are clearly the hardest hit.

As American economic inequality spreads, dangers that Black Americans have long been exposed to are now affecting a larger and larger percentage of White Americans as well. Taken together, these factors leave as many as 50 percent of Americans inordinately exposed to disease and make a unified response to pandemic especially difficult. By nailing down these physical causes of illness, there is at least a hope that in "building back better," (as presidential candidate Biden has put it), we might take these causes and their mitigation into consideration when designing future policy actions. Of utmost importance in our search for answers: how do buildings in the urban landscape contribute to disease – their design, their different uses, their arrangement within districts – and how we move from one to the other. These topics are taken up in turn below.

Density and the "bad habits" of the Black and Brown Americans

Some have argued that residential density is the vector for disease, a premise supported by the early onset of the pandemic in our densest city: New York. A secondary early assumption was that disease was caused by morbidity factors, such as obesity, hypertension, and other health factors that presumably affect those who don't "take good care of themselves."

US Secretary of Health and Human Services Alex Azar was not subtle in implicating the unhealthy lifestyles of minority Americans in an on-air interview with CNN on May 17.

> *"Unfortunately, the American population is a very diverse population with significant unhealthy co-morbidities that do make many individuals in our communities, in particular African American and other minorities particularly at risk here because of significant underlying disease health disparities and disease co-morbidities."* [28]

---

27   (The National Urban League, 2020) Blacks are three times more likely to die of COVID than Whites. This is the same discrepancy between the races as the likelihood of being shot and killed by police. (Schwartz, 2020)
28   (Azar, 2020)

Figure 1-1. The assumed "fever nests" of New York City. Illustrations clearly depicting the abodes of poor Irish immigrants of the day to make the connection between lifestyle, habits, family size, and disease. Illustration from the Healy Collection, NYC.

This sort of remark was not confined to Secretary Azar, nor confined to his time. America has a long history of rushing to blame the lifestyle habits of those below the poverty line, or a presumably unsophisticated ethnic group, for the diseases that befell them. When cholera ripped through Lower Manhattan in the early to mid-1800s, affecting a largely Irish-American cohort, the presumably dissolute habits of the poor were also blamed.[29] It was not until 1854 when a Dr. John Snow of England discovered that cholera was transmitted via contaminated food and water consumed by the poor, and by the waste of cholera victims, that New York's leaders reacted intelligently by upgrading their water and sewer systems.

The best evidence against the contention that it is co-morbidity of minorities which lays them low comes from Great Britain. Great Britain was also hit hard by COVID (highest per capita rate in Europe) and has similar levels of inequality as the US. An exhaustive data dive examining 17 million complete but anonymous heath records of the United Kingdom's National Health Service elicited the following insight:[30]

> *"Particularly compelling were the study's findings on race and ethnicity, said Sharrelle Barber, an epidemiologist at Drexel University who was not involved in the study. Roughly 11 percent of the patients tracked by the analysis identified as nonwhite. The researchers found that these individuals — particularly Black and South Asian people — were at higher risk of dying from COVID-19 than White patients.*
>
> *That trend persisted even after Dr. Goldacre and his colleagues made statistical adjustments to account for factors like age, sex and medical conditions, suggesting that other factors are playing a major role.*
>
> *An increasing number of reports have pointed to the pervasive social and structural inequities that are disproportionately burdening racial and ethnic minority groups around the world with the coronavirus's worst effects."*[31]

Latino and African-American residents of the United States are three times more likely to become infected than their White neighbors and three times as likely to die.[32] And yet the preponderance of deaths among minority groups does not correlate with residential density. In New York City, where robust data sets allow researchers to track cases down to the postal code level, we learn that Manhattan, the highest-density borough of the city, and one that is increasingly White and wealthy, has the lowest incidence of COVID cases, while lower-density outer portions of

29   (Garner, 2015)
30   (Williamson, 2020)
31   (Wu, 2020)
32   (Oppel, 2020)

the Bronx, Queens and Brooklyn, areas with a higher concentration of Blacks and Latinos, have much higher levels of infections per capita.

Low-income as the vector for disease

What best explains this concentration of disease among minority populations, if not density, lifestyle or special susceptibility? Low-income seems to be the driver. The low-income of Black and Brown Americans relative to Whites is a disparity that has persisted since the 1950s, despite dramatic increases in minority education levels.

In 1968, just 54 percent of Black adults had a high-school diploma. Today, 92 percent do. Just 9 percent of Blacks had a college degree in 1968. Now, 23 percent do.[33] And yet average wages for Blacks remain stuck at just 51 percent that of Whites nationwide.[34] This shocking difference is partly caused by including in this depressing statistic the number of both Whites and Blacks that are no longer in the labor force, due to unemployment, not actively looking for work, or incarceration. Blacks have a proportionately higher percentage in all three of these categories.[35]

Obviously low-wages, in and of itself, is not the vector for disease. Susceptibility must be somehow tied to the activities and life choices associated with this low-income, i.e. the job itself or the housing you can afford given that salary.

Black Americans, as one might expect given these low levels of income, are inordinately represented in low-wage service industries, including jobs in retail, food services, cab drivers, bus drivers, warehousing, delivery, hospital nonprofessional staff, and so on. The proportion of these low-paying but essential jobs held by Blacks is twice that of Whites.[36] Current research has shown that holding down these "non-relocatable jobs" exposes workers to higher COVID risks.[37]

Conversely, the percent of professional, managerial, and financial services jobs, i.e. "relocatable jobs", held by Blacks is proportionately less than half that of Whites.[38] During the 2020 pandemic, most "non-re-locatable" service jobs were considered newly "essential" (such as grocery clerks). Thus, these inordinately low-wage workers could not either work from home or stay home and still pay the rent.

---

33 (Brooks, 2020)
34 (Leonhardt, 2020)
35 This suggest the tie in between COVID and the urgency of criminal justice reform.
36 (Salsberg, 2018)
37 (Baker, 2020)
38 (US Bureau of Labor Statistics, 2012)

Given that neighborhoods in New York (where the best data comes from) are highly segregated by ethnicity and income, residents with a high likelihood of becoming infected had similarly endangered persons on their streets, in their cafés, and on transit, adding to the risks of exposure they experienced each day.

The complex system of inequality and disease

Proving disease is "caused" by just one or even two contributing factors is impossible, although correlations are much more than suggestive. For example, minorities, again because of lower-income, are more likely to lack health insurance than Whites. Even more odious is that the health-care system has structural inequities between Black and White patients even when they have similar health care plans. A New England Journal of Medicine editorial puts it this way: "Slavery has produced a legacy of racism, injustice, and brutality that runs from 1619 to the present, and that legacy infects medicine as it does all social institutions." [39] In a Washington Post follow-up article spawned by this editorial, Tina Douroudian, an optometrist in Sterling, VA expresses evidence of subtle and systemic racism this way:

> *"I ask all of my diabetic patients if they have ever seen a registered dietitian," she says. "The answer is an overwhelming 'yes' from my White patients, and an overwhelming 'no' from my Black patients. Is there any wonder why they struggle more with their blood sugar, or why some studies cite a fourfold greater risk of visual loss from diabetes complications in black people?"* [40]

Thus the relationship of disease to income and location in the urban fabric is, as we can see, multi-faceted. But to conclude that breaking down and alleviating geographic inequality for minorities would improve health outcomes is strongly supported by the evidence.

Infrastructure, race, poverty and disease

Infrastructure decisions have also been identified as contributing to the inordinately high COVID death rates among Blacks. Robert Moses,

---

39   (Evans, 2020)
40   (Russell, 2020)

according to Robert Caro's famous biography of the man, intentionally pushed for disruptive limited-access highways through New York's largely minority neighborhoods. He even, in some cases, ensured that clearance heights on bridge overpasses would be too low for buses, presumably carrying the poor, in order to keep Long Island beaches largely White.[41] That strategy was not unique to New York or Moses, but was typical in other cities and regions as well. Close-in "streetcar" neighborhoods were plowed through by freeways in many cities to give ready auto access to newly developing and almost entirely White suburbs. The result is that poorer close-in neighborhoods are typically subjected to harmful air quality, which leads to a higher incidence of asthma, ultimately resulting in higher COVID death rates. The effect is not insignificant. A paper from the Harvard School of Public Health reports that "for every one

Figure 1-2. Low clearance overpass on the Belt Parkway in Brooklyn. According to Biographer Robert Caro, Robert Moses built parkways for cars only, to limit access to low-income riders presumably in buses. Image: Google maps.

microgram per cubic meter of pollutants added to the air we breathe there is an 8 percent increase in mortality from COVID."[42] Many low-income neighborhoods located next to heavily used freeways have over 8 micrograms of pollutants per cubic meter. Robert Bullard, a professor of urban planning and environmental policy at Texas Southern University and author of *The Wrong Complexion for Protection: How the Government*

41   (Caro, 1974)
42   (Harvard School of Public Health, 2020)

Response to Disaster Endangers African-American Communities,[43] and nine other books on the relationship between race, cities and the environment put it this way:

> *"'Oftentimes, communities of color have the wrong complexion for protection,' Bullard said in an interview with NPR's Weekend Edition Sunday. 'You can't wash race out of it ... There's all kinds of studies that show that race is still the most potent variable for predicting who gets more than their fair share of the 'nasty stuff,' and who gets more than their fair share of the good stuff.' Bullard argues that losing out on 'the good stuff' ultimately shortens Black and brown lives. Minorities are disproportionately likely to live in areas with more pollution and in areas that are flood-prone."*[44]

Figure 1-3. Typical medium density "streetcar suburb" street in the predominantly Black East Flatbush neighborhood where disease hit hard. This is not anyone's image of high density life. Image Google Maps.

The political polarization of urban form

The tendency to blame health conditions on cities and density seems almost rooted in the DNA of American culture. An anti-urban bias can be traced back at least as far as Thomas Jefferson's utopian rural vision: a paradise of righteous rural farmers, far from the corrupting hierarchies of

43   (Bullard, 1991)
44   (Valentine, 2020)

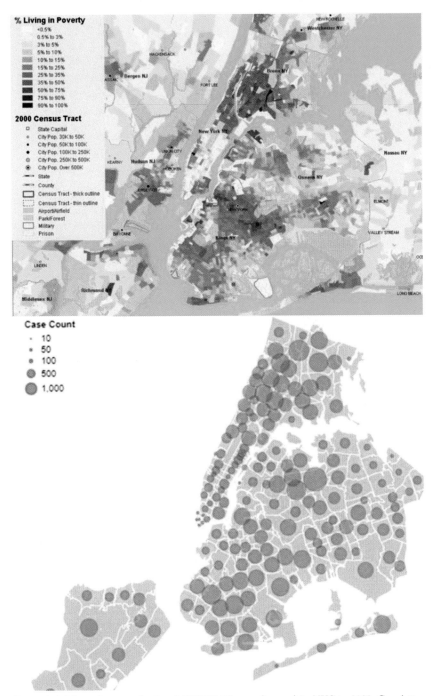

Figure 1-4. Maps of poverty (top) and COVID-19 cases (bottom) in NYC in 2020. Correlation between income status and disease is fairly clear. Illustrations from Brooklyn Magazine (data source US Census Bureau).

the city. Jefferson imagined yeomen farmers as the mainstay of a "bottom up" democracy operating largely at the village scale.[45]

A direct line from his 18th-century premise to the 20th-century claims that helped drive the suburbanization of America (and similarly characteristically American claims for the salubrious effects of low density on both character and health) can also be convincingly drawn.[46] This cultural conflict between walkable density and auto-oriented sprawl, or between urban areas and rural areas, has only become more extreme in the 21st century. The political affiliations of Americans now seem largely dependent on which side of the urban/rural divide one resides.[47] American political polarization is not so much a function of living in a red or blue state, or rich vs. poor, but rather the difference between living in a walkable urban area or in auto-oriented sprawl, regardless of the state.[48]

This urban/rural divide is also markedly in evidence when rural dwellers and city dwellers are asked their views on the 2020 pandemic. The Gallup polling organization discovered a marked difference between rural dwellers and urban dwellers in how they reacted to the pandemic, with 66 percent of urban dwellers taking precautions by March 19, 2020 and only 42 percent taking similar precautions in rural areas (regardless of state). This split was a near-exact correlation with party affiliation split, with 65 percent of Democrats taking precautions against infection compared with 43 percent of Republicans.[49]

Civil unrest, the city and disease

During the spring of 2020, in the midst of some of the darkest days of the pandemic, Derek Chauvin, a White Minneapolis police officer, kneeled on the neck of George Floyd, a 46-year-old Black man, until he died. Caught on camera (as all things are these days) the video sparked riots, then nationwide protests involving both Whites and Blacks (and every skin shade in between). In some ways, the middle of a plague seemed an unlikely time for throngs of protesters to hit the streets. In another way it made perfect sense. As Frederick Reilly put it in his July 8, 2020 USA Today op-ed:

---

45   (Wood, 2002)
46   (Jackson, 1985) Jackson's book, Crabgrass Frontier, has become a classic anthropological study of the motivations behind the unique appearance of the American suburb and its connection to the American rural mythos.
47   (Florida, 2013)
48   (NYTimes, 2018)
49   (Saad, 2020)

Figure 1-5. A Black Lives Matter "die-in" over tram tracks, protesting alleged police brutality in Saint Paul, Minnesota (September 20, 2020). Image: Fibonacci Blue via Wikimedia commons.

"Communities of color are disproportionately ravaged by COVID-19. Communities of color are also bending and breaking under the weight of decades of structural racism — our country's "unfinished business" — which impacts not only how policing and criminal justice are meted out but also how our educational, economic and health systems function by design.

At the same time, we know that the health and economic toll of this period will cut a wide path across America, leaving vulnerable communities of all colors and stripes in its wake. At times like this, facing multiple perceived threats, our local communities and our country as a whole may struggle mightily to secure and strengthen our "bonds of affection." It's natural, it's human, to let fear divide us. It takes heart and courage to tap the deep waters that connect us." [50]

Racial inequality is now seen as the most odious manifestation, and a structural one, of inequality more generally. However, the combination of the plague and the Black Lives Matter protests in 2020 indicates that this time, the outrage against systemic inequality extends beyond the Black community.[51] Unlike previous American race protests, where

50 (Riley, 2020)
51 (Washington, 2020)

participants were virtually all Black, this time people of all colors participated and in some cities, Seattle for example,[52] White faces predominated. This is less surprising than one might initially think, when one realizes that the pressures on White wage earners are now, if not equal to the pressures on American Blacks, are beginning to resemble them, especially for Americans under the age of 40 (Millennials and Generation Y).

Since 1980, mean American wages have remained flat (in inflation-adjusted terms) while the costs of fundamental life-supporting goods such as education, health care and especially housing have more than doubled (also in inflation-adjusted terms).[53] Housing costs in booming coastal cities are even worse, quadrupling since 1950.[54] Access to these necessary fundamentals are increasingly out of reach at levels enjoyed by Baby Boomers and even Generation X. This intergenerational inequity is undermining not just health. Social stability is also undermined.

The first strong evidence of broad discontent with inter-generational inequality was seen in the Occupy Wall Street protests that started in New York and quickly spread throughout the developed world. Before the rage subsided, protests were held in more than 80 countries.[55] Here again, the protesters were largely White and young, and for the first time

Figure 1-6. Occupy Wall Street protest, September 2011. Photo by Paul Stein.

---

52   (Gutman, 2020)
53   (Martin, 2017)
54   (Fidler, 2019)
55   (Taylor, 2011)

in modern history, a worldwide protest movement was sparked by purely economic issues and economic class was redefined as the "one percent" against all the rest. Their complaint was, and is, that the wage earners (and wage earners are the lion's share of the 99 percent) were gaining a smaller and smaller portion of the economic pie, while the investor class (the 1 percent) were grabbing too much.

Their diagnosis is correct. For the three decades after WWII, the share of product value (be it for a car or an insurance policy) going to wage earners stayed steady at about 60 percent of sale price.[56] [57] After 1980, despite massive worker productivity gains in the intervening decades, the wage share of value has dropped to around 40 percent, with the remainder going to owner/stockholders. This is hugely significant as it means trillions more dollars are going into the pockets of those who need it least, i.e. the small class of Americans with sufficient capital to invest. Enthusiasts for this system on the political right claim that the broader population benefits from this system in that retirement plans and consumer-accessible mutual funds are also lifted up. Unfortunately, as generous corporate retirement plans become rarer and as housing and other essential costs proportionately rise, the capacity of average Americans to invest is much reduced. More than 50 percent of Americans now have a negative net worth, and very few below the fifth quintile (those in the top 20 percent of income) have a significant net worth (beyond the value of a home should they be lucky enough to have one – and again, Millennials don't). The average member of the American middle class now has only $4,000 in retirement savings, [58] enough for one month's rent for a two-bedroom apartment in San Francisco.

The COVID plague is making this discouraging diagnosis grimmer still, as the bottom 50 percent of Americans are decanted into districts where housing is offered at prices that, if not exactly affordable, are at least possible. As this sorting takes hold with ever-greater ferocity, the same infection dangers experienced by American Blacks and Latinos expand to include a larger number of Whites as well.

Taking a look now at just one state (where the data is fairly robust at the time of this writing), Massachusetts, we can chart the incidence of infection and death against the average income levels of the state's cities and towns. Massachusetts is a geographically small state with well over

56 (Piketty, 2014)
57 (Zaveri, 2020)
58 (Horowitz, 2018)

Figure 1-7. Aerial view of Fitchburg Mass, one of the state's poorest cities. 78 percent White, 5 percent Black. Highest infection rate in the state in May, 2020. Image : Nick Allen Wikimedia commons.

home to primarily lower-middle-income and low-income residents (largely older former mill towns). Of the 10 richest towns in the Commonwealth, the average COVID infection rate is, as of this writing, less than 1 percent.[59] In the 10 poorest cities, the average rate is more than four times higher. In Newton, the richest city,[60] the rate was .66 percent. In the poorest, Springfield,[61] the rate was over 6 times higher at 4.25 percent. Fitchburg Mass, also on the list of top ten poor communities, had an even higher infection rate at 4.9 percent. Yet the population of Fitchburg is only 5 percent Black and 78 percent White. This suggests that low-income in economically segregated areas is the vector for COVID infection, not race by itself.[62]

The conclusion is inescapable. For the average Black family, the vector for the disease is low-wages. Low-wages correlate with high-contact service jobs that cannot be conducted from home. It also correlates with concentration of low-wage earners in highly income-segregated areas where those in your neighborhood are similarly endangered and will endanger each other in cafés, on sidewalks, at work and on transit.

---

59   (Data USA, 2020)
60   (Sparkes, 2019)
61   (Mass. Department of Public Health, 2020)
62   (Data USA, 2020)

Housing cost, education, the city, and disease

It is the cost of housing that is sorting residents by income into narrowly bracketed communities, and thus concentrating those at highest risk. Sadly, income segregation is getting more extreme, not less. Research by the Sage Foundation shows that, while schools are not more segregated by race than they were 50 years ago, they are dramatically more segregated by income. Families are moving to communities with better schools and amenities if they can afford it, leaving behind people of all races who can't. Such dramatic increases in the degree to which urban regions are segregated by income are shown to impede academic achievement for all races in disadvantaged school districts.[63] The aforesaid educational challenges can thus be added to the health challenges of residing in lower-income districts. A nationwide sorting of Americans by income and occupation type, against the background of what is commonly referred to as a housing crisis, can now be seen as especially damaging to the security, health, and educational well-being of the nation. It is a threat that is not

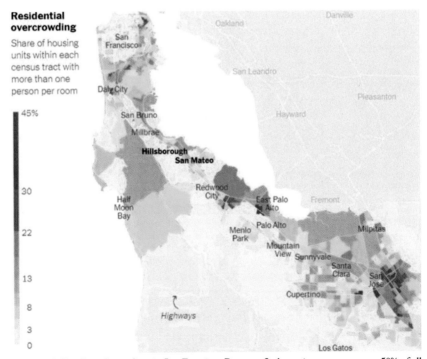

Figure 1-8. Residential crowding in San Francisco Bay area. In lower income areas over 50% of all rentals can be crowded. Data US Census Bureau.

---

63   (Duncan, 2011)

only clinical in its cause and cure, but which should also, if we are reasonable, be addressed by reconsideration of our increasingly inequitable economic geographies.

Building type and disease

But what of the housing type itself? What evidence links our public and private choices around housing type to communicable diseases? At the beginning of the 2020 pandemic, much concern was expressed about high-density buildings and the possibility of shared spaces (elevators,

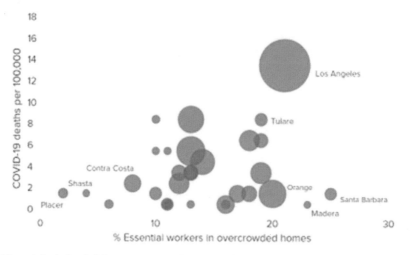

Across counties, there is a clear link between COVID-19 deaths and workers in overcrowded homes

Figure 1-9. A clear link between overcrowding, essential work, and deaths in the state of California is demonstrated in this chart. Source: Image from Public Policy Institute of California.

lobbies, hallways, and common rooms) spreading the disease. At the time of this writing, the evidence strongly suggests that residential density, in multi-unit buildings, is not by itself the problem. Models of droplet behavior provided by Richard L. Corsi, dean of engineering and computer science at Portland State University and a specialist in indoor air quality, suggest that given slow rates of air exchange in elevators, droplets from an infected person can linger in elevator air long enough to infect the next rider; but this is pure hypothesis.[64] On the other hand, Dr. Ilan Schwartz, assistant professor of infectious diseases at the University of

---

64   (Parker-Pope, 2020)

Alberta, notes that the infection rate for family members living with an infected person is only 10 to 20 percent, much lower than the infection rate for measles at 70 to 90 percent.[65] One would expect that if one can catch COVID from a 10-second exposure in an elevator, living with someone who has it would be deadly.

Living with others in close quarters is proving far more deadly than sharing elevators, it seems. Work from the Public Policy Institute of California shows a clear link between apartment crowding, occupations deemed "essential workers," and deaths. Across the nation, the rate of overcrowding is relatively low at under 5 percent (overcrowding defined as more than one occupant per room). In California, due to the severity of the housing crisis there, the rate is 8.3 percent state-wide. But for low-wage "essential workers" in the agriculture or food industry, the rate is much higher at 24 percent, with some lower-income communities showing a rate of over 40 percent.[66] And California counties with the most crowding, such as Los Angeles County, also experienced the highest COVID death rate.[67] Again, due to the nature of this complex epidemiological problem, crowding alone is not a proven singular "cause" of death, but exists within a multivariate context-driven largely by ever-in-

Figure 1-10. Typical Westlake Los Angeles apartment block. Westlake has the most severe overcrowding in Los Angeles. Image: Creative Commons.

---

65   (Ibid.)

66   (Dougherty, 2020)

67   (Meja, 2020)

creasing inequality.

Transport, the city, and disease

Finally, we come to the confounding issue of how transportation mode influences the transmission of disease. In the early days of the US pandemic, focused largely on New York City, many people associated New York's particularly early and severe health crisis with its unique-in-the-US subway system. It seemed logical that crowded subways, along with high-density neighborhoods, were vectors for the disease. Early work, such as the widely disseminated study by MIT's Jeffrey E. Harris, "The Subways Seeded the Massive Coronavirus Epidemic in New York City," reinforced that view.[68] His title was far more inflammatory than the article, within which Harris was careful to avoid any claims of causation or

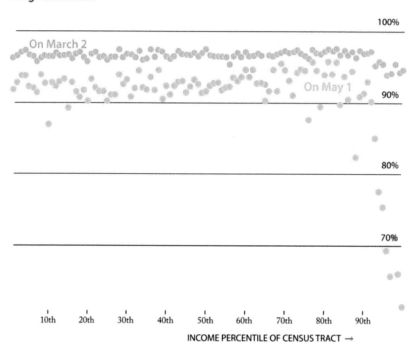

Percent of N.Y.C. residents who were home, in poor and rich neighborhoods

Income percentiles reflect those in New York's five boroughs.

Figure 1-11. Percent of New Yorkers who left the city at the peak of the pandemic by income percentile. Data from Descartes Labs.

68   (Harris J. E., 2020)

to even narrow down correlations to one influence only. Nevertheless, the pre-publication (pre-peer review) release of his paper, prompted by his apocalyptic title, caused an eruption in the media.[69] Reaction from urbanists was swift. Salum Firth, director of the Urbanity Project at George Mason University in Georgia, did an equally deep dive into the same data to come to the opposite conclusion: cars were the culprit. [70] Firth's conclusion seems counterintuitive. How could sitting in your own car by yourself be an occasion to catch or spread disease? The answer seems to be that neither subways nor cars are the vector. Inequality is. Firth pointed out that there was a higher correlation between auto use and disease and subway use and disease; but left largely unremarked by him was the much stronger correlation between inequality and disease evident in the data. Indeed, over 40 percent of Manhattan residents in the top decile of income (top tenth) simply left town to wait out the plague. New Yorkers in the bottom nine-tenths of income did not have that option, nor were they rich enough to live in most of Manhattan.[71] They were instead sequestered in the moderate- and low-income boroughs far from Manhattan where disease was concentrated and where they were exposed to danger regardless of how they got to work.

Conclusion

Inequality more than any other factor is the vector for pandemic. This inequality is manifest in where a home is located, how much it costs, how many people live within it, what job types are associated with what type of resident, and how concentrated within the district are families with similar characteristics. Systemic racism, both blatant and more subtle, have placed Black families in proportionately much higher danger than White families. However, systemic income inequality is increasingly placing wage earners of all races in similar danger. The social tensions spawned by systemic inequality and racism are now manifest in eruptions such as the Black Lives Matter protests and the earlier Occupy Wall Street protests.

Inequality in housing is far more odious than in more benign forms. Housing is a basic for life. Citizens can't really choose not to pay for a home. Paying the Rent must come first. In this way, paying the Rent is

69   (Harris D. J., 2020)
70   (Furth, 2020)
71   (Quealy, 2020)

unlike paying for a flat-screen TV, double-shot latte, or avocado toast. This makes the doubling of average home prices nationwide, and the more than tripling of housing costs in jobs-rich coastal cities, particularly problematic. Urban designers and those forging urban development policy now have an additional reason to address housing and urban form inequities. More than just social justice is at stake. National health and even national security are now on the line. In the following Chapters, we will illustrate practical short- and long-term solutions used as correctives.

Chapter 2

The Problem of wealth, capital, and urban land

Introduction

The contention that the pandemic is exacerbated by inequality is probably beyond dispute. It might also be fairly said that for many of those afflicted, the illness was caused by inequality: in income, systemic racism, the jobs assigned to lower-income Americans, and inadequate and limited housing choices. This volume, however, focuses on what city development policy can do about all of this. Thus, this chapter will focus on why housing costs too much. As mentioned in the introduction, the problem of inadequate housing is, in its most essential form, a problem of wages that are too low competing for housing that is too expensive. While design and planning policy have relatively little influence over wages, design and planning policy have quite a bit of influence over housing cost. Consequently, that will be the focus of this chapter.

Is the housing market the problem, or is it the solution?

Essentially, when it comes to the question "why does housing cost too much?" there are only two responses. The most common is that if planners would allow for more housing construction the "laws of supply and demand" would ensure that housing costs would drop. The second response is that, believe it or not, more supply won't automatically fix the problem.

The first response has the advantage of conforming to all the lessons taught in most introductory microeconomics courses. Those who offer the contrary position, having no generally accepted law to use as a cudgel, start off on their heels. This is because belief in the "invisible hand of the marketplace" and the "law of supply and demand" have held sway in the planning discourse since at least the '80s, and those who argue otherwise are dismissed as NIMBYs[72] or worse. Only in the last decade has widespread allegiance to free-market ideals eroded. The commonly accepted theory of supply and demand has been undercut by the observed reality; i.e., that no matter how much a metropolitan area adds new housing units, housing prices continue to rise. This begs the question: If the high price of housing is not caused by constrained supply, what is the problem? The problem seems to be the cost of land.

The cost of land

It is helpful to remember that there are three determinants of real-estate value: location, location, location. Tired as this aphorism may be, it is no less valid for it. The truth is that it's not the house you buy (or Rent), it's the dirt under it. And that dirt, or location, can't be moved. Accepting this, it follows that it is not the cost of the building that is crucial (construction costs, adjusted for inflation, have not risen that much in 20 years), it is the cost of the land the building sits on. This is true even for high-rise buildings on small parcels, because if not for the location, and the value it provides, no high-rise would rise. Thus, you can only lay claim to land you can afford, and increasingly urban Americans can't afford much. Geographic inequality regimes are established, enforced, and extended by the price of urban land. Many claim that this landscape of inequality is just the consequence of the invisible hand of the marketplace in action, and to interfere with the market smacks of socialism. But urban land has no value except for the value it passively absorbs from the public actions occurring around it. It's not the invisible hand that gives land its value, but our collective actions unfolding around that land over time. Given that, it may seem reasonable to distribute that value to the

---

72   NIMBY: Not In My Backyard. A pejorative reference to residents who oppose any changes to their neighborhoods, no matter how necessary.

advantage of those who have collectively generated that value; i.e. the urban public. This is not how the urban land market works. That value is largely captured by the lucky owners of urban land.

These lucky, or smart, landowners are the beneficiaries of what economists call David Ricardo's "Law of Rent," defined in his 1817 *On the Principles of Political Economy and Taxation*.[73] In simple terms, the "Law of Rent" means that the price paid to the owner of land (in his time that was typically the lord of the manor, or the "landlord") by the user of land (in his time that would be the farmer who had to rent the land) was equal to the difference in productive value between productive land and land used for the same purpose that was worthless. Ricardo's law states that every penny of the difference in that value will go, not to the farmer who reaps that bumper crop, but to the landlord. This view of the ability of landlords to passively acquire value produced by others is the accepted way that economists think of land rent, or more broadly of land price (which is technically just another version of land "Rent"). The Law of Rent is more important for urban uses than for farming. The most productive land in a city is land at the center of all the services and infrastructure needed to maximize productivity. For clarity, and for simplicity, in this volume when the term rent is used in this Ricardian sense, it will be capitalized as rent. To illustrate how land rent and racial inequality are linked, we start with the most obvious historical example of how government policy can either grant or deny land rent to entire races, providing a brief recap of the troubling 150-year history of withholding land wealth from African-Americans.

Racial exclusion from land

Some of what follows is relatively well known, but it bears repeating. At the time of this writing, African-Americans own, on average, only one-tenth of the wealth claimed by the average American White ($17,000 vs $170,000).[74] Most of the capital value held by American Whites is in the form of urban land (largely their fully or partially paid-off home). The current low comparative wealth of America's Black families is a legacy of slavery. After the American Civil War, and despite the exhortations of abolitionists, no serious effort was made to redistribute land to freed slaves.

---

73   (Hawes, 2010)
74   (McIntosh, 2020)

The history is complex and multifaceted, but the failure of one initiative stands out as especially unjust. That is the failure of the "Freedman's Bureau."[75] Set up at the end of the Civil War and with President Lincoln's support, the Bureau's goal was to distribute land to former slaves. The amount specified was 40 acres each (or a quarter-quarter section in the parlance of the Continental Land Survey).[76] Importantly, the land to be redistributed was land that had been "abandoned, or to which the United States shall have acquired title by confiscation or sale, or otherwise." Originally the act (as administered during Lincoln's life) would have "confiscated" White-owned plantations, with land parceled off to the freed slaves who had worked it. After Lincoln's assassination, President Andrew Johnson (a Democrat from North Carolina), quickly reversed course. Henceforth, southerners who signed a "loyalty oath" would have confiscated lands returned to them, ensuring that White plantation owners would reclaim the south's most arable lands. Blacks also had to compete with White "refugees" for what lands remained. Then, to make it completely impossible for Blacks to claim land, White owners quickly instituted vagrancy laws (without federal objection), making it a crime for Blacks to be idle, giving them no choice but to work for the same "masters" to whom they had been enslaved.[77]

One more thing: Simultaneous with the Civil War and the later failed Freedman's Bureau initiative in the south, the federal government was opening up western lands for settlement under the terms of the "Homestead Act." The act was designed to give free land to Americans in the western plains (and eventually beyond). The land was sparsely (in modern terms) but not entirely unoccupied. These lands were former Spanish colonies or Native American lands.[78] These free farmsteads were theoretically available to the newly freed slaves. A small number of freed slaves were able to take advantage of this initiative and were able to acquire land. Unfortunately, most southern Blacks were, after Lincoln's death and in light of the prohibitive race laws passed by southern governments, no more than indentured servants, under "contract" to work plantation lands. Breach of contract would result in jail terms, with prison labor served on the same plantation lands, but this time for no pay.

Comparing the results of the Homestead Act to those of the

---

75   (Cox, 1958)
76   The Continental Land Survey, and its impact on the American urban and rural landscape, is brilliantly described in *Measuring America*, by Linklater (Linklater, 2002)
77   (Daniel, 1979)
78   (Arrington, 2012)

Freedman's Bureau makes for a disheartening comparison. Relatively few of the 4 million southern Blacks ended up with land, either in the south or western plain states, while 4 million Whites got free land under the Homestead Act. As Kerry Leigh Merritt, author of *Masterless Men: Poor Whites and Slavery in the Antebellum South*[79] points out:

> "*The number of adult descendants of the original Homestead Act recipients living in the year 2000 was estimated to be around 46 million people, about a quarter of the US adult population. If that many White Americans can trace their legacy of wealth and property ownership to a single entitlement program, then the perpetuation of black poverty must also be linked to national policy. Indeed, the Homestead Acts excluded African Americans not in letter, but in practice – a template that the government would propagate for the next century and a half.*"[80]

Racism, housing, and land wealth in the 20th century

Again, in brief, because much of this is well known and others cover this ground more completely, institutional racism has blocked access to real-estate wealth for Blacks up to this day. Just after the Civil War, three constitutional amendments were passed: the 13th abolishing slavery, the 14th affording due process protection to Americans of all races, and the 15th guaranteeing the right to vote regardless of race. Amendment 13 is the best known but less known is that section II of that amendment gives Congress (still to this day) the right to pass laws ensuring state compliance. Congress followed up in 1875 with its "Civil Rights Act" barring all discrimination, public or private. Sadly, in 1883 the US Supreme Court declared that in passing this law, Congress had exceeded the authorities granted by the 13th Amendment, arguing that it did not give Congress the right to rule over the use of private property. In 1896, the Supreme Court went even further in its landmark Plessy v. Ferguson decision, declaring specifically that "separate but equal" facilities, this time including public schools, were constitutional. These Supreme Court precedents would not be overturned until 1968 when the case of Jones vs. Myer came before the high court. Joseph Jones was an African-American who

---

79   (Merritt, 2017)
80   (Merritt, 2016)

sued the Alfred Meyer Company for blocking his purchase of a new home in St. Louis because he was Black. The decision effectively reversed the Plessy vs. Ferguson interpretation of Amendment 13 almost 100 years after the 13th Amendment passed. [81]

While prior to 1968, private developers such as William Levitt (the builder of the famous "Levitt Towns") were free to refuse home sales to African-Americans, for city officials intent on keeping White neighborhoods white, things were slightly more complicated. Cities and towns throughout the US were free to institute explicitly discriminatory zoning codes (setting aside certain parts of town for Whites only) until 1917 (the year when the Supreme Court outlawed the practice in its Buchanan vs. Worley decision). Undeterred, many US cities continued the practice, including Palm Beach (till 1960), Kansas City (till 1987) and Norfolk, Virginia (until 1987).[82] And finally, when all else failed, cities and towns could simply use zoning rules set to ensure that the vast majority of Black families (having been successfully blocked from capital accumulation for a century) could not afford to move to their town. Setting high minimum lot area requirements (five-acre minimums were common) was a common tool of "de facto" racial discrimination and class exclusion.[83]

This practice endures to this day and the battle rages on. The Obama administration sought to address this inequity in the mildest of ways, issuing an order requiring suburban communities to offer a plan to end this kind of race and class discrimination as a condition for receiving federal funds of all types. He acted as the executive administrator of the Fair Housing Act of 1968 in this instance.[84] The "Affirmatively Furthering Fair Housing" executive order would require suburban communities to show that their housing policies conformed to the 1968 Fair Housing Act.[85] Failing to do so would impede access to federal funds. During the 2020 US election, President Trump made this order a centerpiece of his

---

81   (Rothstein, 2017) Rothstein's book was depended on for much of this section and is considered the authoritative contemporary source for this history.

82   (Ibid.)

83   (Babcock, 1973)

84   The Fair Housing Act (as it is commonly known) was passed with a substantial bipartisan majority (65 southern Democrats in the House voted no). It was rushed to the floor of both houses two weeks after the assassination of Martin Luther King, with President Johnson twisting arms. It gives citizens the power to sue private entities in the case of discrimination. Sadly, the act has been ineffective due to lack of enforcement. Housing advocates estimate that to this day there are between two and four million violations annually, (National Fair Housing Alliance, 2008) most of which remain unresolved. The Obama executive order was issued in 2015 and intended to take enforcement out of the hands of individuals, poorly equipped for this role, and charge municipalities to pro-actively address this issue instead. Failing same, municipalities would lose the federal funding in various categories that they may have been counting on. The Obama administration argued that this is a simpler and more effective means to ensure compliance with the act. Trump disagreed.

85   (Fuchs, 2020)

campaign, promising to kill the rule, and thereby hoping to re-instill racist fears among White suburban residents. He claimed that candidate "Biden will destroy your neighborhood and your American Dream. I will preserve it, and make it even better!" [86] At the time of this writing, it is

Figure 2-1. Typical discriminatory 5-acre minimum sprawl zoning in Sudbury Mass. Image from Google maps.

not clear if this fear-mongering still resonates. American suburbs have become increasingly mixed. The White share of US suburbs fell by 8 percent between 2000 and 2018, and now stands at 68 percent (and is trending toward rough parity).[87] Unfortunately, as mentioned previously, this mixing of races has not been accompanied by improvements in Black wealth share. African-Americans still possess only a tenth of the wealth, on average, of White Americans.

What we already know about the pandemic, national responses, and racial wealth trends

While at the time of this writing, the long-term economic effects of the 2020 pandemic are not entirely clear, certain things are already obvious. Since job losses in the US have hit low-wage workers hard, and low-wage

---

86 (Olorunnipa, 2020)
87 (Parker, 2018)

Black and Brown workers even harder,[88] these cohorts are experiencing ever greater financial stress. Absent continued federal requirements to extend generous unemployment support, continue mortgage forbearance, and continue various limits on evictions from rental units, housing security for low- and moderate-income Americans is further endangered. And avenues to gain land wealth are further blocked. Meanwhile, efforts to keep America's corporations from collapsing led the Federal Reserve and Congress to inject trillions to protect shareholders (most shares are held by the upper 10 percent of Americans).[89] Money went out in the form of low- to no-interest loans (financed with newly created money from the Federal Reserve Bank) to everything from airlines to real-estate investment trusts (REITs), protecting both rental unit landlords and the portfolios of the investor class.[90]

While this approach is reasonable in the short-term, economists disagree about what to do over the longer term. Their approaches range from center-right to center-left positions. On the political right, they recommend pumping more and more newly printed money into the pockets of the investor class, up to and beyond the point where inflation returns (based on the principle that keeping corporations healthy saves jobs). Economists of the center-left are more inclined to suggest rebuilding by shoring up the purchasing power of wage earners, and to do so by reinvigorating unions and creating new entitlements to put wage earners in a stronger bargaining position with their bosses (strengthened in the knowledge that even losing a job you would retain robust federally insured benefits).[91] America's best-known Nobel Prize-winning economists Joseph Stiglitz[92] [93] and Paul Krugman[94] promote the second of

---

88   (Luhby, 2020) While more Black and Brown people were in the ranks of low-wage "essential workers" and thus more endangered, they were also at least twice as likely to lose their jobs as Whites.

89   (Wigglesworth, 2020) Americans in the top decile of income own 90 percent of all stock. Americans in the top centile captured all of the growth in stock wealth of the previous 10 years.

90   (Ocasio-Cortez, 2020) REITs were granted taxpayer funds to maintain employment. Contention arose around requests to use taxpayer funds, in the words of Ocasio-Cortez, "to artificially inflate stock prices, enrich shareholders, or compensate executives with exorbitant pay packages when so many hard-working, ordinary Americans do not know where their next paycheck will come from and in too many cases are ineligible for stimulus checks or unemployment benefits."

91   (The Economist, 2020) This analysis depends in part on an Economist magazine "Briefing: A new era of economics" in the July 25th, 2020 issue. In this article, they in turn depend on the scholarship of Anna Stansbury and Lawrence Summers, both of Harvard University, in their conference piece "Declining Worker Power and American Economic Performance" (Stansbury, 2020).

92   (Hepburn, 2020) Stiglitz et al. suggest that given infrastructure deficits and rising inequality, it is wise to spend money on building 21st-century infrastructure to put money in pockets of workers rather than propping up financial markets.

93   (Stiglitz, 2020)

94   (Krugman, 2020) Saying things like: "I hereby propose that the next US president and Congress move to permanently spend an additional 2 percent of GDP on public investment, broadly defined (infrastructure, for sure, but also things like R&D and child development) — and not pay for it."

these two options. It follows that a more robust governmental involvement in housing would align with the center-left economic response by shoring up the security of wage earners, allowing wage earners to change jobs with a much-reduced fear of homelessness, and this time clarifying that housing is critical national infrastructure.[95]

Millennial Whites increasingly also closed out of land wealth

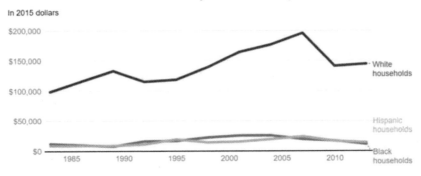

Figure 2-2. The median net worth of Black Americans is only 10 percent that of Whites. Modest gains made between 1990 and 2007 were wiped out by the real-estate crash of the Great Recession. Most White wealth is in the form of homeownership. Homeownership has built multi-generational wealth for White families through inheritance but not for Blacks. Data Pew Research Center.

The pandemic has also revealed that geographic inequality, the vector for the disease, is a problem increasingly shared by White Americans, particularly those under the age of 40. Younger Americans of all races, particularly those living in jobs-rich coastal cities, are experiencing daunting gaps between the cost of housing and what they can afford. In all of the US, both home purchase prices and rents have more than doubled in the last 20 years (on average).[96] In some coastal cities, prices have quadrupled.[97] But these raw price increases don't tell the whole story. Those who already own homes, older on average than those looking to purchase their first home, escape the worst.

---

95   (Fearn, 2014) Transportation, clearly considered by all to be infrastructure, is the other half of a pair with housing. The two are symbiotic. Odd that they are not yet universally considered as paired elements of a common infrastructure.
96   (Martin, 2017)
97   (Fiddler, 2019)

In fact, those lucky enough to have purchased their homes 20 or more years ago are, again on average, sitting on substantial wealth gains (and are naturally loath to see them reduced). But absent very dramatic decreases in home prices (no one seems to want that, least of all the Federal Reserve or recent buyers), and absent a doubling of wages for those under 40 (the trends there don't look promising, to say the least), home-ownership or even reasonable rents are increasingly out of reach for younger Americans.

That is, of course, unless Millennials have free access to "the bank of mom and dad" for the six-figure down payment required (which is, increasingly, the only way for young people to get on the first rung of the US home equity ladder).[98] Again, much of this is generally known but a few facts to support such broad assertions are merited. Millennials with some college or a high-school diploma are making roughly 85 percent as much, in constant dollars, as Baby Boomers.[99] And even though Millennial college graduates are making 9 percent more (again in constant dollars) than Baby Boomers,[100] they carry an average of roughly $40,000 in educational debt into their first professional job.[101]

But that's not all. The average Baby Boomer also carries about $40,000 in educational debt.[102] What gives? Are those 60-year-olds going back to school in huge numbers? No, they are obligating themselves through the "Parent PLUS" student loan program and others like it to finance the huge costs of their children's education.[103]

These unprecedented educational debts explain why the average net worth of Millennials is 36 percent lower ($8,000) than that of Generation X at a similar age. That figure is itself skewed by our breathtaking inequality levels which allow a Mark Zuckerberg, whose 2020 estimated $86 billion in net worth would equal the average net worth of more than 10 million of the roughly 80 million Millennials.[104] Because of these unprecedented strains, Millennials are putting off (or giving up on) marriage and childbirth by six years on average,[105] having fewer children on

---

98   (Martin, 2019) In 2019, 43 percent of American Millennial home buyers got money, needed to qualify for mortgages from parents. Previous generations were much more able to finance their home on their own.
99   (Balk, 2019)
100   (Ibid.)
101   (Stolba, 2019)
102   (Ibid.)
103   (Ibid.) Parents taking out loans to support their kids' college expenses is laudable, but it begs the question: What about young Americans whose parents don't qualify for these loans? It suggests yet another roadblock on the path to upward mobility for financially disadvantaged Americans.
104   (Duffin, 2020)
105   (Stahl, 2020)

average (1.7 per female and trending down, far below replacement rate of 2.1),[106] living with their parents at nearly twice the rate as in the year 2000 (rapidly accelerated by the pandemic),[107] and putting off (or giving up on) purchasing a home (they are half as likely to own a home by age 35 as were Baby Boomers).[108]

These financial constraints are showing up in indicators for pandemic risk not unlike those experienced by American minorities: accepting more crowded living conditions due to high housing costs (half of Millennial employed in the "essential workforce" spend more than 30 percent of pretax income on housing),[109] higher likelihood to be employed in the high-exposure service gig economy, and fewer opportunities to work from home (college-educated Millennials may do so in large numbers to be sure, but only 39 percent of Millennials have college degrees).[110] Generally speaking, the massive growth in precarious jobs (otherwise known as the gig economy) are both adding to the risks of the pandemic and limiting opportunities to acquire real-estate wealth, start a family, or secure a comfortable retirement. [111]

The gap between housing and income

The connection of racial and economic inequality to unequal risk for disease seems unassailable. It is worthwhile for housing advocates, planners, and designers to understand the economic drivers behind trends that currently exacerbate inequality for both minorities and the youth of all races. The causes, and therefore the solutions, are not obvious and have confounded policy professionals for decades. A majority of policy-makers hold firm to a faith that the inherent power of the housing market to supply affordable housing could be unleashed if restrictions on density were removed. Evidence from after the 2008 economic crash does not support this faith. The basic problem seems to be that wages are essentially flat while housing prices, in both rigidly regulated jurisdictions and those less so, have risen out of sync with wages. [112]

For at least the five decades since WWII, housing economists have

---

106   (Editorial Board, 2019)

107   (Pinsker, 2020)

108   (Thompson, 2014)

109   (Freddie Mac, 2019) "Nearly half of households headed by people ages 18 to 34 are rent-burdened, meaning that more than 30 percent of their paycheck goes to their landlord."

110   While a higher percent of Millennials have a bachelor's degree or higher than previous generations, that figure is still only 39 percent. (Balk, 2019)

111   (The Prudential, 2019)

112   (Knoll, 2014)

assured us that a region's housing market is structurally linked to a region's average wages. And that even if the market could not effectively house those in the bottom 20 percent of income, the free market was best suited to supply housing for the rest. However, in many US cities, particularly cities on the jobs-rich coasts, the relationship between regional wages and average house price has been cut. What was once a dependable ratio of average wage to average home price of 1 to 4, is now roughly 1 to 8 and more than 1 to 12 in many coastal cities. And sadly, efforts to increase housing supply in the laudable hope that doing so will satisfy demand, and thus lower prices, does not seem to work. Houston, which is famous for operating without zoning controls, saw a five-year jump in average home prices of 27 percent between 2013 and 2018,[113] while wages grew well below the rate of inflation at 1.9 percent in 2019.[114] It seems

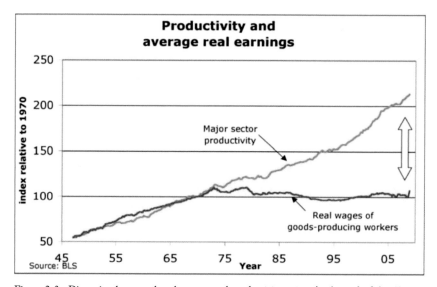

Figure 2-3. Digression between hourly wages and productivity gains. At the end of the 60s you see that productivity and wages, previously growing in tandem, split, with all future gains going to capital. Information Bureau of Labor Statistics. Image: Wikimedia Commons.

that home-price increases no longer rise and fall with region-wide salary levels. But home prices in major US cities do rise and fall in line with the rise and fall of housing prices in similar global cities. Since at least 2000, when the price of homes in New York or San Francisco go up, so too do

113   (Silver, 2019)
114   (Douglas, 2020)

prices of homes in London, Sydney or even Shanghai.[115]

What gives?

Well, according to the Federal Reserve Bank of Dallas, the problem is not the cost of the house. The problem is the cost of the land it sits on. A quote from their report, "Globalization and Monetary Policy Institute Working Paper No. 208", is worth sharing here:

> "*This paper presents annual house price indices for 14 advanced economies since 1870. Based on extensive data collection, we are able to show for the first time that house prices in most industrial economies stayed constant in real terms from the 19th to the mid-20th century, but rose sharply in recent decades. Land prices, not construction costs, hold the key to understanding the trajectory of house prices in the long-run. Residential land prices have surged in the second half of the 20th century, but did not increase meaningfully before.*"[116]

Why are urban land prices no longer linked to average wages? Well, there seem to be two different but related ways to explain this confounding trend. The first explanation, now quite popular, suggests that this gap between wages and housing costs is simply one aspect of inequality more generally. The second explanation, a variant of the first (now being revived after a 100-year hiatus), is that urban land has a special ability to absorb value, in the form of land Rent, until it becomes no longer affordable by the average wage earner. Below we start with the first explanation and a few pages later provide an explanation of the second. The two explanations are, as you will see, compatible and systemically linked.

Growing inequality as the problem

While policy makers disagree on the cause, everyone, be they on the political left or the political right, agrees that inequality in the US is increasing – dramatically. Wages are flat but most everything you really need to buy costs more: housing, cars, education, stocks, health care, etc.

The most popular explanation for this trend comes from center-left

---

115   (Ibid.)
116   (Knoll, 2014)

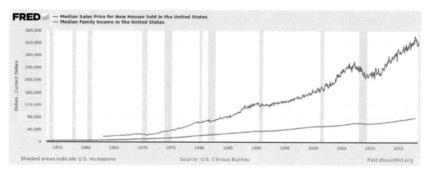

Figure 2-4. Rise in median US Family income vs average home price. Home prices double since 2000 with wages up only 50%. In jobs-rich coastal cities home price increases are much greater.

French economist Thomas Piketty. In his widely read and hugely influential first book, *Capital in the 21st century*,[117] he explains that given the fundamental mechanisms of capitalism, unless interrupted, wealth will naturally gravitate toward those who already have wealth and away from those who live on their wages. This tendency eventually results in a "patrimonial capitalist" end state. That's where a small number of wealthy (now often called oligarchs) and their descendants exert near-monopoly control over both the economy and the politics of a nation. Like all good economists, he provides a mathematical formula to explain all this: R > G, where R is the generally constant (throughout the centuries) 5 percent return on capital (Rents, interest, etc.),[118] and G is the rate of GNP (gross national product) increase.

Piketty claims that when GNP grows faster than 5 percent, there is enough new wealth created such that wage earners can increase their wealth share (relative to the investor class, that is). He takes over 600 pages to prove his point, so beyond this the writer will simply direct those interested to his book to absorb his argument there. However, one key point made by Piketty should be repeated. He asks and answers the question: Why is it that during the '60s, '70s and '80s, the proportionate share of total capital wealth controlled by America's and Europe's middle class was increasing? And why, on or about 1980, was that trend reversed? His answer is that the three great catastrophes of the early 20th century, WWI, the Depression and WWII, played a role by bombing the factories of the rich, by raising their taxes to 90 percent of income, and by rendering their bonds worthless through wartime and post-war inflation.

---

117   (Piketty, 2014) Piketty's book sold over 10 million copies worldwide. No book on economics has come close since Progress and Poverty in 1879.

118   While the decade post-2008 has seen interest rates on treasury notes (and other guaranteed return instruments) below this level, returns on stocks and real estate have been higher than 5 percent over the same period.

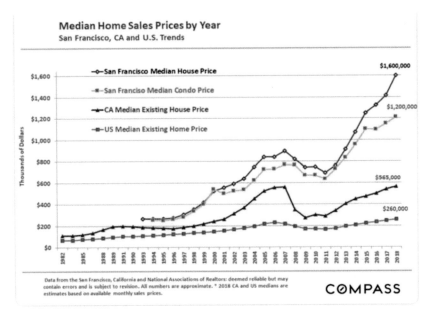

Figure 2-5. Home price increases in San Francisco vs. California vs. US. Jobs-rich coastal city housing prices far outstrip wage increases. Data: National Association of Realtors.

This post-war financial restart allowed advanced nations to rebuild rapidly (or in the case of the US to capitalize on their new global dominance) with very high GNP growth, higher than 5 percent per year for decades.[119] But all this came to a stop in the late 1970s during the period of "stagflation," a time when Keynesian[120] economic approaches seemed to fail. This set the stage for the "Reagan Thatcher Revolution," [121] initiating a shift back to "neoliberal" or "neoclassical" unfettered "free market" economic approaches. In Piketty's view, this set up the machinery of the global economy to slowly produce greater and greater inequality, levels of inequality akin to levels experienced during the "Gilded Era" of the late

---

119   GDP growth has not averaged (10-year averages) over 5 percent in decades. Post-2009 recovery has been particularly weak at between 2 and 3 percent a year (Jones, 2020). If Piketty is correct, this helps explain why inequality increased dramatically after the 2008 "Great Recession."

120   Keynesian approaches (named for British economist Milton Keynes) generally signify approaches to managing a nation's economy wherein the government aggressively intervenes, typically willing to spend itself into deficits to keep the economy humming. The 2020 pandemic made even the most ardent neoliberals into instant Keynesians.

121   (Dadkhah, 2009) The "Reagan Thatcher Revolution" is shorthand for the historical moment when both economies (US and British) turned away from "Keynesian" interventionist economic theory, and returned to former "classical economic" theory of laissez-faire and minimal government intervention into the economy, an approach promoted by Thatcher favorite Friedrich Hayek and others like him (notably Milton Friedman in the US). The term neoclassical economics is often used interchangeably with neoliberal economics. They both align in many key respects, notably on the primacy of the "free market." The differences are not crucial here, except to say neoclassical economics emerged earlier and is associated with microeconomics while neoliberal emerged mid-20th century and is associated with macroeconomics.

19th century. [122]

In Piketty's second book, *Capital and Ideology*,[123] he takes a deeper dive (at 1,300 pages, much deeper!) into political and economic history, to conclude that the groundwork for what the French call the "Three Glorious Decades" (1950-80) was actually laid in the late 19th century, by the political foment of the Progressive Era in the USA,[124] and by the various socialist movements on the continent. During this period, wage earners increased their power vis-a-vis the investor class (via public support for labor unions and for a steeply progressive income tax in the US, for example) and via the beginnings of a government-sponsored social safety net (retirement benefits in the UK, for example).

At the end of WWII, the ground was set, he illustrates, for the emergence of strong social democracies in Europe and for the continuation of New Deal policies in the US.

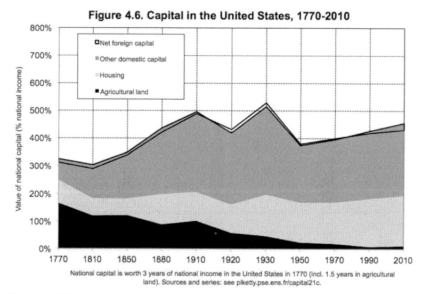

Figure 4.6. Capital in the United States, 1770-2010

National capital is worth 3 years of national income in the United States in 1770 (incl. 1.5 years in agricultural land). Sources and series: see piketty.pse.ens.fr/capital21c.

Figure 2-6. The value of urban housing (primarily land value) represents a growing share of all capital value (as a ratio of annual GDP) in the US and is the largest single category of American wealth. From "9 charts that explain the history of global wealth." Note amazing decrease in wealth share of agricultural land vs housing. Charts adapted from (Piketty, 2016).

122   (Piketty, 2014)
123   (Piketty, 2020)
124   (McGerr, 2003) The Progressive Era (1890 to 1920) influenced many aspects of contemporary American political and economic life. Notably, it was during this era that four constitutional amendments were passed, the 16th (the income tax), the 17th (direct election of senators), the 18th (prohibition), and the 19th (the vote for women). Henry George, although he passed away earlier, is often given credit for amendment 16, the income tax amendment, advanced by his son Congressman Henry George Jr. and his political ally Warren Bailey. Originally very little of the US income tax applied to ordinary wage earners. It fell almost exclusively on the rich. Not so today.

He sums up by saying that post-1980 globalization led to an unfortunate relaxation in financial controls around the world, setting off a competitive race to the bottom where owners of capital got taxed less and less while austerity politics undercut the relative power of wage earners (undercutting trade unions and shrinking supports for the social safety net).

So what does all this mean for housing prices? It means that cheap and plentiful money, in the hands of the investor class, has bid up the exchange value of all asset classes (gold, stocks, bonds, and land). Of these asset classes, the single biggest (and growing) proportion of investment capital has flowed into, and thus has bid up, the price of urban land.

The mechanics of urban land value as the problem

The second explanation for the failure of the market to supply affordable housing, even in the absence of zoning constraints, has to do with land Rent. Modern economists use the word "economic rent" as wealth that does not derive from productive capital (a factory for example), but rather derives from a locational, monopoly, or risk-mitigation advantage of some kind. This definition makes "economic rent" a difficult concept for the layperson to understand. For example, both wage increases negotiated by labor unions and the advantages of monopoly control over, well, anything really, are considered economic rent. Joseph Stiglitz, Nobel economist, uses the example of "too big to fail" banks[125] as an example of a risk-mitigation advantage. When the federal government agrees to bail out banks with taxpayer money, which produces a shift in value from the public to the private sector, owners of bank shares see the value of their holdings increase in line with their reduced risk (this type is called "rent seeking" because you lobby for it)

But this definition of economic Rent muddies the waters.[126] The original and more obvious definition of Rent remains valid, particularly for our purposes of deciding why housing costs too much. The more obvious example of "economic rent," and the one that interests us as planners and urban designers, connotes the yearly cost to use the land, or the amortized yearly cost to buy land (which usually amounts to roughly the same thing).[127] Land Rent is the cost paid by a land user to a landowner for

---

125   (Piketty, 2015)
126   (Gaffney, 1993)
127   (Ricardo, 1817)

putting the land to some purpose.[128] Why do we care about separating land value, or land wealth, from other kinds of wealth? We care because knowing the amount of land Rent lets us separate that cost from the costs of both productive capital (like a factory) and labor (wages) necessary for production. Land in this view is necessary but only contributes to production by virtue of its location. Land, in economic terms, is "worthless" without labor and capital to put it to use.

Unfortunately, the value of land, this inherently "unproductive" form of property has, in the terms most often used by American economists, been conflated with the worth/utility of "productive" property, such as factories or apartment buildings. This has reduced the commonly understood ingredients necessary for economic production down to only two: capital and labor. Joseph Stiglitz maintains that neoclassical economists,[129] made a serious error (perhaps by design) when they conflate productive capital with unproductive land, calling both "capital," and rendering land's essentially parasitic aspect invisible to economists (Marxists do the same).

The idea that land is not productive, dates back at least to the time of Adam Smith's work The Wealth of Nations, where he says:

> *"As soon as the land of any country has all become private property, the landlords...love to reap where they have never sowed, and demand a rent even for its natural produce. The wood of the forest, the grass of the field, and all the natural fruits of the earth, which, when land was in common, cost the laborer only the trouble of gathering them, come...to have an additional price fixed upon them."* [130]

Smith here sums up an issue that after 250 years is still important. The "landlord," as he correctly puts it, monopolizes the use of land (demanding Rent) without providing any capital (factory) or labor (work) value. In this view, land, which could under ideal circumstances be available free of charge to the factory owner and her workers, absorbs some or most of the value of capital and labor in the form of land Rent. Most modern economists try to overcome this objection by merging factory value

---

128   Sometimes the owner and the user are the same person, and GNP calculations include an "imputed rent" in their calculations to acknowledge this reality.

129   (Hayek, 1944) Hayek, in his famous and polemical book The Road to Serfdom, came out in opposition to Keynesians prior to WWII, and picked up adherents among the investor class as advanced economies faltered in the 1970s. He skillfully linked laissez-faire capitalism with personal liberty in a way that appealed to political conservatives.

130   (Smith, 1776)

with the value of the land below, assigning them both productive value. Stiglitz complains that this "economic rent" for land, if not mitigated through controls such as state ownership or taxing policy, exacerbates wealth inequality by draining off the productive value of both productive capital and labor into the value of land.[131] As this process of value absorption unfolds, more and more value gets absorbed in the Rents for urban land until the productive capacity of productive capital and labor are overwhelmed. More odious still, because of the way that land markets work, the price of land (its Rent) can temporarily be pushed beyond the capacity of labor and capital to afford the land price. That's when crashes, like the one we experienced in 2008, happen. Indeed, when looking back at American economic history it is significant that American economic depressions/recessions over the past 140 years were often preceded by an urban land price bubble.[132]

For Stiglitz to make this claim is not surprising. The work upon which his reputation was founded was based on land Rent. In what came to be known as his "Henry George Theorem",[133] he explained that investments in city infrastructure (in the broadest sense, inclusive of roads, parks,

Figure 2-7. Seven year increase in land value by zip code. Los Angeles Metro. Land prices in central LA area increased by over 450% in only seven years.

---

131 (Piketty, 2015)

132 The "Great Depression of 1929"was preceded in 1926 by a real-estate correction (Nicholas, 2013). The "Long Depression" beginning in 1873 was triggered by the collapse of a speculative market in land around new railroads (Lee, 2008). That bust in land prices stimulated Henry George to understand the damage done to both labor and capital by uncontrolled privatization of land. Professor Gaffney, Henry George scholar (Gaffney, 1993), explains how land price drives recurring recessions thus: "Bank credit swells and shrinks in sync with the land cycle… buyers need more credit to purchase land; the appreciated land then serves as collateral for more bank loans until the paper value of land brings down the "real" economy. Real-estate crashes wipe out equity that banks and individuals depend on to stay solvent. Crashes increase foreclosures that damage bank solvency, which freezes up capital markets leading to business failures and associated consumer retrenchments, ergo recessions like the dramatic 2008 Great Recession. This is why many notable contemporary economists blame land speculation for business failures and unemployment, a theme that echoes the diagnosis of Henry George."

133 (Wikipedia n.d.)

hospitals, schools and so forth) would be reflected in the total land value of the area served, and that quite often land value increases were larger, in the aggregate, than the level of public investment would seem to warrant. Thus, public investment is a productive producer of wealth; i.e. taxpayer paid civic infrastructure more than pays for itself as reflected in increased land values. What follows from this is that public sector investments should be financed by a heavy tax on that element that benefited most from those investments, and the main beneficiaries are the owners of urban land. Acquiring funds from taxing land to extend and enhance civic infrastructure would allow governments to reduce taxes on capital income, sales, and wages; reduced to reward and encourage these useful categories of economic activity. Thus, a tax on land value should be the primary means of financing public infrastructure (again broadly conceived). His work is called the Henry George Theorem because it was Henry George, an American autodidact economist of the Progressive Era, who first promoted this idea.

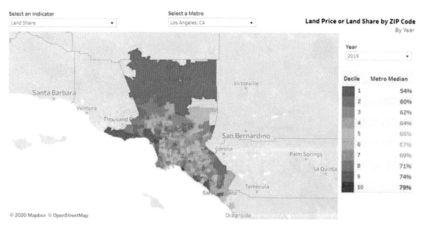

Figure 2-8. Land share of total parcel value. Data American Enterprise Institute.

The Importance of Henry George

Henry George was a journalist turned political economist who worked in California in the 1870s. It was while doing that work he was struck by an insight, recounted in his seminal work, *Progress and Poverty*: [134]

---

134   (H. George, 1879)

"For, as soon as land acquires a value, wages, as we have seen, do not depend upon the real earnings or product of labor, but upon what is left to labor after rent is taken out; and when land is all monopolized, as it is everywhere except in the newest communities, rent must drive wages down to the point at which the poorest paid class will be just able to live and reproduce, and thus wages are forced to a minimum fixed by what is called the standard of comfort — that is, the amount of necessaries and comforts which habit leads the working classes to demand as the lowest on which they will consent to maintain their numbers."

George describes a world where more and more of the returns to capital and more and more of the pay envelopes of wage earners go into land Rents (paid to landlords or banks), leaving workers with just enough left to "live and reproduce." The situation experienced by Black Americans and increasingly by White Americans described in previous pages seems to conform to his bleak description – minus the reproduction part, it seems (birth rates among young Americans are currently below replacement rate).

Henry George is almost forgotten in the world of economics, overtaken by Marxism on the left and neoliberal and neoclassical economics[135] on the right. But during his lifetime he was a revolutionary figure, more famous than Mark Twain and of much greater impact than Karl Marx. He deserves more attention than he gets, for unlike Marxists and socialists, and unlike neoclassical conservatives, George escapes the seemingly irresolvable ideological dead end of class warfare between capital and labor.

Both the intellectual left and the intellectual right largely see the worker and the owner in an endless fight for their fair share of wealth. Those on the right feel that workers should be grateful for the wages that the "job creators" provide, regardless of how much their efforts enrich the owners. Those on the left see owner's profits as unjust, constituting a theft of the "surplus labor value" of their work. Combatants in both camps ignore the fact that much of their combined efforts go to fill the pockets of landowners in the form of Rents. Henry George puts both owners of capital and wage earners on the same team, happy to leave both labor and capital largely untaxed to place that burden where it belonged, on the

---

135   (H. George, 1900)

landowner who extracted monopoly (because land can't be moved) Rents without adding to production. Or as Adam Smith so elegantly put it so long ago, on "the landlords. . . . (who) love to reap where they have never sowed, and demand a rent even for its natural produce."

Socialists of Henry George's time held a similarly dim view of "landlords." But their prescription, nationalization of the land, was more extreme than that of Henry George. George would simply shift taxes from both wages (income taxes) and capital (business taxes) and apply a greater tax to land, commensurate with its nonproductive value, its Rent. This strategy made George a unique and revolutionary figure in his time, neither socialist nor neoclassical capitalist, but one who clearly separated out the non-productive element of capitalist society, i.e. land Rent, and strategically targeted land Rent value for taxation to be used to eliminate economic disruptions caused by speculation – such as the one experienced in 2008 – while providing funds for the common good. Freeing the economic machinery of the dead weight of land Rents, he claimed, would reduce the frequency and severity of depressions. He explained that the recurring cycle of economic depressions (that were a relatively new feature of life in his times) were caused by land Rents. Landlords, by their nature, always pushed capitalism to the brink of failure by demanding maximum Rents. At these unsustainable levels, economic disruptions (like the collapse of the real-estate bubble in 2008) meant that capital owners (entrepreneurs) could not keep up with the Rent and lowest-paid workers (labor) would then be on the streets. The knock-on effects were inevitable, he said. Over-leveraged individuals and banks would see their equity collapse, while their liabilities could not be rolled over. Result: depression.

For years, George's book *Progress and Poverty* was the only book in the US that outsold the Bible, selling millions of copies, and translated into over a dozen languages.[136] That was a feat unheard of for a book on political economy (at least until the publication of Thomas Piketty's *Capital in the 21st century* in 2014).[137] His insights spawned a movement in the English-speaking world, leading significantly to Progressive Era

---

136   (George, 1900)
137   (Piketty, 2014)

Figure 2-9. Mayoral candidate Henry George strangling a large snake wrapped around New York City Hall. The snake represents "corruption," "monopoly," "rings," "deals," "spoils," "nor law," "club law," and "want." On the ground is a club emblazoned with the title of George's famous book, *Progress and Poverty*. Image: Wikimedia commons.

constitutional amendments in the US and land tax policy in the UK.[138] His renown was such that he stood for election as mayor of New York City in 1886, and would have won had it not been for vote tampering by Tammany Hall. For the first time, states and cities throughout the US and Canada adopted separate property tax valuations for "land" and "improvements," due to his work. Most US states established "Single Tax" political groups to advance his ideas, many of which still exist. Henry George spawned US think tanks that still thrive from financial legacies seeded by his followers. But his own work was halted by an untimely death due to stroke when he was just 58 years of age.[139]

Part of the reason for George's diminished standing is due to the

---

138   (P. Jones, 1987) From the abstract: "Henry George, the American social reformer and Single Tax advocate, made six visits to Britain in the last quarter of the 19th century, a period crucial in British labor politics. George became locked in contest for the minds and hearts of British working men and women, as well as all classes, with the advocates of Christian and moderate socialism and with Karl Marx and Frederick Engels, the chief advocates of State Socialism (a.k.a. Communism). Though it was Marx's adopted country, George won out for a time, and it was his program for competitive capitalism, with socialization limited to industries unsuited for market discipline, which influenced development of a mixed economy."

139   (H. J. George, 1900)

powerful forces arrayed against him, powers that were invested in maintaining and extending the wealth they had acquired from Rents. Most powerful among those interests were the fantastically wealthy railroad barons of his day, whose wealth derived largely from land. This debate was lengthy, vicious and complex, and profoundly political as well. Those wishing for the complete history should read "Neo-classical Economics as a Stratagem Against Henry George" by Mason Gaffney for the full recounting.[140] Here we touch only on the fact that Columbia University and the "Chicago School" of economics at the University of Chicago were set up, and staff hired, for the specific purpose of refuting Henry George[141] (faculty unwilling to do so didn't last long). As Gaffney points out, academic attacks on George at the behest of the very wealthy were sustained and vicious:

> *"George was also in a running dispute with E.R.A. Seligman, Chairman of Columbia's Department of Economics over many, many years (circa 1880) under both Presidents Low and Butler.….. Butler, in turn, was the funnel through which the wealth of Wall Street, personified by the dominating banker J.P. Morgan, patronized Columbia, making it the wealthiest American university for its times. Money poured into the Department of Economics under Seligman, his Department swelled from two members to "forty or fifty"… This was a period of secularization of US colleges. Businessmen were replacing clergymen on boards. The new broom swept out some old problems, no doubt. At the same time, it posed new threats to academic freedom, threats of which Butler was the very embodiment. Clerics, after all, owe some allegiance to Moses, the Prophets and the Gospels, which are suffused with strident demands for social justice. They were displaced by others more exclusively attuned to the Gospel of Wealth. Academic tenure was a distant dream: top administrators hired and dismissed with few checks and balances. They only needed to dismiss a radical occasionally: others got the message . . . Pressures on academics were extreme: it was placate or perish."*

---

140   (Gaffney, 1993)
141   Not just these two but others of a similar orientation: Ezra Cornell (owner of both Western Union and Associated Press) – founder of Cornell University; John D Rockefeller – helped fund the University of Chicago and installed his allies in its economics department now known as "The Chicago School"; J. P Morgan – investment banker and early funder of Columbia University; B&O Railroad – John Hopkins University, Southern Pacific Railroad – Stanford University

Henry George didn't precipitate a violent revolution like Marx, or set the terms of the Cold War like Friedrich Hayek, [142] but his successes were numerous and terribly relevant to our issue of housing costs. His separately assessed and rated property tax on land has been used in 15 Pennsylvania municipalities for over 100 years. The state of Maryland and 28 other states assess land and improvements separately as part of their state-wide tax policy.[143] What is most interesting about this approach is that it leads to reasonable policies that provide a synthesis and a resolution between enthusiasts for the free market and those who are outraged by the plight of the American minority and youthful wage earners. As Henry George preached all his life, the competitive market should control all but the few things the state does best, while necessary revenue used to build the city and the welfare state should come, as much as possible, from those who gain the most and contribute the least: the landowner.

There is a danger in perceiving this insight in terms that are too simplistic. George's work got compressed down into a rather unfortunate slogan, that of the "single tax" on land. That should not be the only way of applying this concept. The "Henry George Theorem" provides a way of correctly and fairly applying tax policy, such that it falls on those who benefit from collective public action, and can be spent to the benefit of those who contribute to the social and economic life of the city. This revenue can be used to build the most important infrastructure of the city. Coming out of the pandemic, it is clear that housing is the infrastructure we most lack; housing to mitigate the crippling cancer of inequality, with funding derived from land-owning beneficiaries of a well-oiled, and attractive city. In fact, we already do this in modest ways, with examples discussed in Chapter six.

Conclusion

Since the 1980s, in thrall to the neoclassical and neoliberal economists like Friedrich Hayek, whose polemics against government influenced Ronald Reagan and Margaret Thatcher and which were then executed by financial leaders like Alan Greenspan, Americans have accepted as a given that the magic of the market can solve all social ills. Even "third way" Democratic US presidents like Bill Clinton were adherents. The

---

142   (Piketty, 2015) Lecture by Piketty, response by Stiglitz.
143   (Bell, 2002)

unrelenting rise of inequality during this period, and the structural impediments still placed in the way of minority advancement, have undercut the legitimacy of this regime. US politics are certainly changing, with calls for wealth taxes and other strategies to reduce the grip of oligarchs on our national life now legitimized. The second civil rights movement has swung public opinion towards support for structural change to ensure equal opportunity for all Americans. For those involved in planning, building, and maintaining the city, the impact of these changes on how we view our collective project can no longer be ignored. Foremost among those new acknowledgments might be this: the current machinery of the economy ensures that the land of the city will be inequitably distributed to the detriment of our collective clinical health, social equity, and racial justice. For city builders who care, the Archimedes Lever with tremendous power to mitigate these ills is housing, and the land below it. Henry George was not the first to identify the problem of land speculation, but remains the most relevant. More recent economists have come around to his point of view. Global wealth is inordinately flowing, not to stocks, or gold, or financial markets, but to urban land. In the process, holders of this wealth are blocking access to land for those who need it. In certain parts of the world, notably Vienna, public leaders have found simple strategies to manage capital flows for the benefit of residents. Those who make city policy would be well advised to be conscious of how their decisions might unintentionally increase poverty while their city progresses. In the following pages, we will describe how Vienna avoided this trap, and how avoiding the inequitable consequences of ever-inflating urban land Rents are accomplished in many forward-thinking US cities.

Chapter 3

Land, Rent and transport

Introduction

For the past 70 years, the US has spread its population over a vast suburban landscape. Now over half of all Americans live spread out over five times the area of the older center cities that spawned them. This well-known phenomenon is pejoratively known as urban sprawl. However, the relationship of sprawl to land Rent is much less well known. For a limited number of decades, American cities were able to escape the deleterious effects of land Rent by, in effect, creating a new American frontier: the suburb. Part of Henry George's argument resonates here. He argued that "new cities," such as his San Francisco home, were less susceptible than older cities to the economic drain of land Rents. Older cities, he argued, had more time for land speculators to exert monopoly control over land Rents, and thus more time to drain the productive efforts of capital and labor into Rents. It was this insight, that the natural equality he found in the frontier gave way in time to the poverty of established cities, that inspired his first and most famous book *Progress and Poverty*. His thesis was that as the city progresses, it inevitably produces poverty. And for him, the cause of urban poverty was excessive land Rent. Here is a taste of his prose on the topic:

"It is in the older and richer sections of the Union that pauperism and distress among the working classes are becoming most painfully

apparent. If there is less deep poverty in San Francisco than in New York, is it not because San Francisco is yet behind New York in all that both cities are striving for? When San Francisco reaches the point where New York now is, who can doubt that there will also be ragged and barefooted children on her streets?

This association of poverty with progress is the great enigma of our times. It is the central fact from which spring industrial, social, and political difficulties that perplex the world, and with which states-manship and philanthropy and education grapple in vain... So long as all the increased wealth which modern progress brings goes to build up great fortunes, to increase luxury and make sharper the contrast between the House of Have and the House of Want, prog-ress is not real and cannot be permanent."[144]

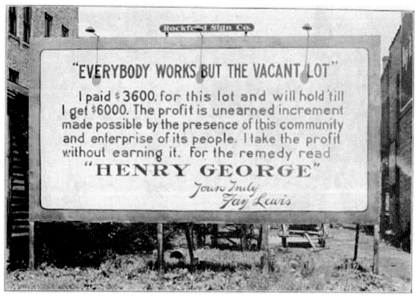

Figure 3-1. Sign spells out in simple terms Henry George's main point. Image from collection of New York Public Library.

Henry George wrote well before the mass production of automobiles and likely could not have imagined how this would, for a time, undercut the monopoly power of urban Rent. But for a few glorious decades it did. With the encouragement of the oil and auto industry and with a massive

---

144   (H. George, Progress and Poverty, 1879)

program of federally funded freeway construction, a vast new American urban "frontier" was opened up. A half-hour drive on this new system opened up sixteen times the acreage contained within the old city limits, and, for a time, made ownership of single-family homes an achievable goal for grocery clerks. Sadly, in time the progress of the '60s turned into the poverty of the 21st century, with Rent pushing housing out of reach for Millennials (or at least those without access to parental cash) and freeways congested to the point that commutes now sometimes took hours. Now this generation finds itself, yet again, the victim of excessive land Rents and suffering through the same levels of inequality that George decried in 1890. To grasp how land use and transportation currently impact our topic of health, inequality, and racial justice it is helpful to look at this legacy of urban sprawl the way economists do.

The economics of the center and the edge

In the previous Chapter, Ricardo's "Law of Rents" was introduced.[145] This law is particularly relevant as a cause of urban sprawl. As the land Rent in urban centers absorbs a higher and higher percentage of the productive value of capital and labor occurring thereon, the incentive to search further afield for lower land Rent increases. The result is urban sprawl.

To illustrate, we return again to our three factors of production: land, capital and labor. Let's imagine five sites for a freestanding Starbucks. The first one is located at the 100 percent central crossroads of our imaginary city. The fifth one is out there on the margin of the metroplex where land Rent is next to nothing, ("worthless" in Ricardian terms). The other three are stretched between them at even increments. Starting with the one at the fringe of the city, to be profitable our owner only needs to sell enough coffee to pay for the building and materials (the capital) and pay for her employees (the labor). Land is not really a factor. So we might put numbers to this as follows: Capital is 5, labor is 5 and land is 0. If they sell 15 units of value the profit is 5 – they stay in business. At the other end of the scale, at the central site the numbers look different. Here she will sell more product, so capital (including the coffee) might be 8, labor might be higher too at 8 but land (Rent) is, as you might expect, much higher at 20 units. In order to reach her profit goals she needs to sell 36 units worth of product just to break even and 41 units to get to her target 5 units of profit. The other three sites pay successively less Rent but also sell less

---

145   (Hawes, 2010)

coffee. Thus, the profit level of each store is the same (and any increases in profits sensed by landlords leads to higher Rents). What this simple example shows is that as you work closer to the center, more and more of the value of the capital and labor goes into Rent, in fact Rent gets most of the value while contributing nothing directly to the coffee business. [146]

Both Ricardo and the earlier Adam Smith understood land Rent as unproductive in these terms, but it was left to Henry George to fully explain its significance. George explained that the "Law of Rents" ensures that land Rents will draw 100 percent of the value a favorable location provides, and will leave only bare subsistence level wages (in the most extreme case) for labor, and precarious profit levels for entrepreneurs. The idea is that wages and profit always stay the same (barely adequate) with any advantage between one location and the next going to Rent.

What the concept of land Rent also explains is that the need to pay Rent affects your calculus about where to locate your business (or home). The higher the Rent the more likely you are to search for more affordable sites further out from the center of economic activity. It also follows that if it were not for the high Rent at the central location, you would be inclined to put your Starbucks across the street from the other one (poaching your neighbor's customers or attracting new ones). The point to underline here is that without Rent, activities would be more highly concentrated at a city center than they are. Those who see land Rents as a major economic driver of urban form also blame land Rents for causing urban sprawl.

Housing and land Rent

The same logic can be applied to the forces that locate housing. High land prices in metropolitan region centers make it less likely that families will be able to afford appropriate housing near the conveniences of city centers or close to jobs, no matter their taste for high-density living. And when planning offices try to mitigate these effects by increasing allowable density, they are often frustrated to find that their rezoning efforts have largely benefited landowners, who pocket windfall gains in land

---

146   This analysis is a distillation of a longer and more mathematical analysis contained in *On Fairness and Efficiency*, by George Miller. The main point he makes is that because of land cost, all of our current economy is always verging on recession. Why? Because land prices are always pushing the economy to the "margins," barely eking out a profit (after paying the rent) no matter how much we sell. (Miller, 2000)

value while the price of homes stays high.[147]

So as in the case of the Starbucks example above, the home buyer (or the developer hoping to sell homes) searches for "marginal" sites that can be brought into use with tiny relative land costs. Again, the point to underline here is that if land prices were not a factor you could expect to see lands close to the center used more intensively for housing, notwithstanding some degree of personal preference for detached or attached forms factoring into individual decisions to be sure.

Figure 3-2. Screen grab form the 1946 movie "It's a Wonderful Life". For a brief few decades Americans escaped the grip of high land Rents thanks to the car and the interstate highway system. A new "frontier" opened up. This time not in the west but in the American suburb.

Transport and land Rent

The land Rent issue described above has influenced metropolitan development in all advanced market-based economies, but in the US it was, for country-specific reasons, quite pronounced. After WWII, the nation, for reasons that ranged from national defense (the more you sprawl the

---

147   Sadly, the evidence suggests that increasing allowable density, as many public officials propose, in order to increase affordability, can have the opposite effect. One study from Chicago drew much attention for providing strong evidence of the counter-intuitive consequence of increasing apparent housing "supply" to meet "demand" and thus lower prices. It did not. It raised per square foot housing prices instead. (Florida, 2019)

harder it would be for the Russians to blow it all up, they said)[148] to economic development policy ("what's good for General Motors is good for the USA," they argued)[149] to encouraging the "American Dream" (see the movie "It's a Wonderful Life" for proof).[150]

Building the Interstate Highway System brought a flood of new formerly "worthless" lands inside the reach of the city where, at least at first, the problem of land price inflation was overwhelmed by new supply and a new limited-access highway system overwhelmed, at least at first, traffic congestion. Cheap land, easy access by suddenly affordable cars,[151] and inducements like the GI Bill, mortgage interest income tax deductions, and the "redlining"[152] of medium-density former streetcar neighborhoods, pushed the urban fringes of American cities out much farther than in other countries. Over time, the average metropolitan density of older US cities dropped, often, (as in the Boston metropolitan area) to less than a fifth of their prewar density levels,[153] undercutting (temporarily) the value of the lands under older residential zones. In some rust belt cities, those inner-city land prices are still low. But in the jobs-rich coastal cities, those former streetcar-served medium-density districts (at least those that escaped the ravages of "urban renewal" in the 1950s to the 1970s) have recovered lost land value – and then some.

Conclusion

Now as we wrestle with the effects of the pandemic, on our heels economically and socially, younger Americans of all races find themselves

---

148   (Quinn, 2001). Surviving a nuclear first strike with at least part of the metropolitan area still functioning was a horrifying event to ponder but it did give impetus for military planners to join with others who favored a lower-density, more spread out, city form.

149   (US Department of Defence n.d.) Charles E. Wilson was Secretary of Defense under President Eisenhower and former CEO of General Motors. The full quote is famous: "For years I thought that what was good for our country was good for General Motors, and vice versa. The difference did not exist. Our company is too big. It goes with the welfare of the country. Our contribution to the nation is considerable," as stated publicly in confirmation hearings before the Senate Armed Services Committee, responding to Sen. Robert Hendrickson's question regarding conflicts of interest. Quoted in Safire's Political Dictionary (1978) by William Safire.

150   The story involves two alternative futures for the main character (played by Jimmy Stewart), one "dystopian" where everyone lives in tenements and appears to spend their lives in jazz clubs, drinking and dancing, while the "utopian" future would have recent immigrants living in new five-room ranch houses on large lots arranged on cul-de-sacs – with no apparent desire for jazz clubs. (Nero, 2019)

151   Cars cost slightly more than three times as much now, in inflation-adjusted dollars, as they did in 1953 (dollars.com n.d.)

152   Redlining was the practice of automatically disqualifying any home mortgage within certain parts of the city in favor of newly developing suburban areas. These were invariably former streetcar-served medium-density zones surrounding the center city. One result was that this housing stock, much of which had been owner occupied, were bought up at low prices by professional landlords, many of whom let properties decline into "slum" status – prime areas for later "slum clearance." (Jan, 2018)

153   (Condon, 2010)

handicapped by a doubly difficult legacy of these post-war trends. First, by land Rents consuming an ever-larger share of income on rentals and mortgages, and second by family budgets straining to pay for the two cars now needed to survive in our sprawling auto-centric metropolitan landscapes. Certainly, the influence of land Rent is not the same everywhere. Land value has increased hardly at all in cities like Cleveland. But land Rents have skyrocketed by as much as or over 400 percent in just a few years in many jobs-rich coastal cities. Low land Rents don't help if you can't find a job. And the progress being made in jobs-rich coastal cities exists simultaneously with evident poverty and homelessness at levels that outraged Henry George over 100 years ago.

It's fairly easy to diagnose these problems. Solutions are more difficult. But there is hope. The sprawling landscape left in the wake of our WWII city-building binge is characterized by a relatively low ratio of actual buildings to serviced lands. Looked at this way, we have a hyper abundance of pipes, roads, and utility infrastructure – oversized in the extreme – in comparison to the buildings served. The possibility of capitalizing on this investment in the future, through infill and adaptation of this urban landscape is obvious. If, that is, all our advances do more than enrich landlords.

Chapter 4

A short history of affordable housing efforts in the US

Introduction

Any discussion of the history of affordable housing in the US is fraught and depressing. So this necessary history of our county's halting efforts towards housing security is blessedly short, with the main focus on the problem of land Rents. First, the issue of the way we treat land as property, and as an asset class.

The financialization of land

As Americans, we take for granted that land is privately owned, and that it was ever thus. Actually no. Up until the emergence of "propertarian regimes" in the 18ᵗʰ century[154] (the phrase is from Thomas Piketty who uses the term in *Capital and Ideology* to identify the legal structures emerging in post-Enlightenment, post US and French revolutionary societies), land was effectively owned by the state (given that the state and the "crown" amounted to the same thing).

In Canada, this sense of common property still exists, with most land still owned by "the Crown," and referred to as Crown Lands, with rights

---

154   The phrase, "propertarian regimes" is taken from Thomas Piketty who uses the term in Capital and Ideology to identify the legal structures emerging in post Enlightenment, post US and French revolutionary societies. The new characteristic of propertarian regimes was the nearly absolute right to property, extending even to ownership of slaves. Landownership, in terms we now take for granted, was first legally protected at this time.

of private ownership only governed by common-law precedents.

Our own American Revolution, often called the world's first "bourgeois revolution," [155] was precipitated mostly by the landed class. Members of the landed class included most of the major names listed among the "founding fathers," including Virginia estate owner Thomas Jefferson. Jefferson began his Declaration of Independence with this stirring first principle:

> *"We hold these truths to be self-evident, that all men are created equal, that they are endowed by their Creator with certain unalienable Rights, that among these are Life, Liberty and the pursuit of Happiness."*

This is inspiring phrasing; but it is worth pointing out that there may be nothing truly "self-evident" about it. It is, in truth, a revolution-catalyzing call to arms intended to fire up public opinion, and a particularly effective one at that.

Jefferson's entreaty came at a time when the Enlightenment had a firm hold on Western thinking. The Enlightenment, we should recall, was a humanist (human-centered, as opposed to spiritually centered, in other words) movement opposed to the deification of both church and kings. Fundamental to this new thinking, and a way of thinking that helped move Jefferson's pen, was the idea of an inalienable human right to property. Jefferson astutely altered a phrasing taken from British philosopher John Locke's *Two Treatises of Government*,[156] within which Locke argued that the true function of the state was to protect rights to life, liberty and property. He asserted therein that all humans had a right to "life, liberty, and the pursuit of estate" with "estate" equivalent to the word property in our more modern usage. Jefferson, ever the astute politician, changed the word estate to "happiness," forever establishing an equivalence between the two, an equivalence that has been reinforced by two centuries of American property law.

Obviously, socialists have long had a problem with this point of view. Property law from a socialist perspective is the primary instrument class uses to perpetuate financial inequality within and between generations. America's answer to this complaint has been redistributive tax policy. Progressive taxes aimed at weakening the power of the wealthy have been

155   (Davidson, 2011)
156   (Locke, 1689)

the main device, especially inheritance taxes, which when first imposed in 1910 were 10 percent, rising to as high as 87 percent between 1940 and 1973. Our maximum inheritance tax rate is currently 40 percent (after bouncing up and down 5 or 10 percent over the past 20 years).[157] Unfortunately, land Rents have largely escaped an assault by redistributors, missing a chance to redirect Rent toward social purpose.

Thus, American efforts to provide affordable housing have largely streamed public funds from other sources; to buy land for housing, to grant tax subsidies to developers in return for affordable housing units, and to provide cash subsidies to qualified renters to help them pay private-market rents. All three of these strategies have, unfortunately, forced governments to compete in the marketplace with other entities desiring urban land, and thus increasing Rent. These often troubled efforts are discussed below.

Early starts

Prior to the 20th century, US governments did not assume any responsibility for housing. Earlier government efforts took the form of building-code regulations aimed at preventing egregious fire and health hazards common to 19th-century tenements.[158] Housing supports for wage

Figure 4-1. One of the last remaining textile mill boarding houses in Lowell, Massachusetts, on right; part of the Lowell National Historical Park. Image: Wikimedia Commons.

---

157   (WIkipedia n.d.)
158   (Bauman and Biles, 2000)

earners, where they existed at all, were sometimes provided by factory owners. The case of Lowell, Massachusetts is instructive. Lowell factory owners built an industrial town inclusive of worker housing: dormitories and apartments separated by gender, marital status, and job status. Charles Dickens, in comparing the Lowell industrial city to the depravations in British industrial areas of the time, viewed the occupational and social structure of Lowell much more favorably (in his *American Notes*).[159] But in the rest of the US, providing housing for workers was extremely rare, a task left entirely to landlords in the private sector.

Garden Homes Milwaukee

It was not until late in the Progressive Era that government got involved. In 1916, Milwaukee voters elected socialist mayor Daniel Haon, a position he held till the 1930s. He had campaigned on a platform of housing for "workers," and followed through with a complicated plan for what, in essence, would be a housing collective, with land owned in common by residents. Complications arose and the housing, and the land below, was eventually privatized, but the utopian ambitions of the district and its 200-plus detached homes are still evident in community form.[160] The project was inspired by the British "Garden City" work of Ebenezer Howard, with many of its streets named after British Garden Cities of the day. The district is now on the National Register of Historic Places.

Figure 4-2. Garden Homes Historic District, Milwaukee, Wisconsin, National Register of Historic Places. Image by Freekee, Wikimedia Commons.

Stein and Wright

In the '20s and '30s a number of more robust attempts to provide more affordable housing options were made. Most notable were projects

159   (Dickens, 1842)
160   (Wisconsin Historical Society n.d.)

undertaken by Clarence Stein in partnership with Henry Wright.[161] Both were members of the Regional Plan Association of America (RPA), a private nonprofit planning group serving primarily the New York tristate region. RPA also counted Louis Mumford and Benton MacKaye among its members. Stein and Wright developed numerous housing projects, well known for trend-setting innovations, particularly for adapting housing districts to the car and for providing immediate access to green space from every home. The most famous of their projects is in Fairlawn, New Jersey. Their project, named Radburn, is famous for what is still known as the "Radburn Plan," i.e. a housing district set within a large plot of land bounded by a ring road (this condition is also known as a "superblock") from which cul-de-sac roads extend to serve individual houses. This allows the non-street facing side of the structure to face a green space instead of a conventional street.

Less well known and a point to emphasize here is that the land under the structures was collectively owned, with each resident taking ownership of a share of the land along with property rights associated with their housing unit. In modern terms, this arrangement is known as a "bare land condominium" (bare land strata in Canada), where detached

Figure 4-3. Aerial view of Radburn New Jersey, showing cul-de-sacs on one side of homes, and green spaces on the other. Image: Google Maps.

---

161   (Stein, 1957)

buildings might be privately owned while the land under and around them is owned by a condominium association.

Stein and Wright's reputation was such that they were employed to design many similar projects, working together till Wright died in 1936 (only in his '40s at the time). Stein continued to practice into the 1950s, with significant projects, including Baldwin Hills Village, Los Angeles, California, completed in 1942. Stein captured their collaboration in his widely read book *New Towns for America*, published in 1951.[162]

Depression era housing

Greenbelt Communities

Stein and Wright were also active with the Roosevelt administration during the Great Depression of the 1930s, laboring with the housing section of the Public Works Association (PWA). There they worked on

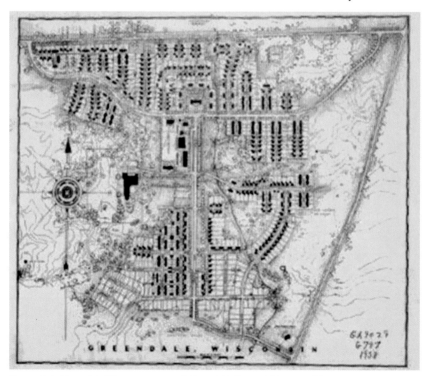

Figure 4-4. Greendale Wisconsin original plan. 1938. Image: Wisconsin Historical Society.

162   (Stein, 1957)

the design of a series of "Greenbelt" communities. The intent was to create complete suburban communities (also inspired by similarly ambitious British Garden Cities), with jobs, housing and civic infrastructure included in the plan. These plans were spatially generous like Radburn, but departed to some extent from the Radburn design. Now home fronts turned decisively toward the street.[163]

Three Greenbelt communities were eventually built: Greenbelt, Maryland; Greendale, Wisconsin; and Greenhills, Ohio. Unlike Radburn and Garden Homes, the land and structures of the Greenbelt new towns were federally owned with commercial and residential tenants paying rent. The strongly "collectivist" structure of these new communities provoked political opposition from the start, leading to the discontinuation of the Greenbelt program only a few years after its start. This is yet another indication of the historically fierce opposition in the US toward any effort to extract residential land from private ownership.[164] After WWII, the federal government privatized the Greenbelt communities, selling residential units to former tenants.

The first housing "projects"

Figure 4-5. Greendale Wisconsin project area today. Image: Google maps.

---

163   The Radburn plan created what is known as the "front door back door problem." At Radburn, the architectural language and floor plans of homes placed the formal "front" side of the home toward the green spaces. This looked fine but meant that visitors who typically arrived by car at the "back" of the house would enter through the mud room and kitchen. Not a satisfactory way to greet your minister.
164   (Williamson, 1987)

Once the Greenbelt program was safely killed, the federal govern-ment adopted what was then a somewhat more palatable strategy: direct financial assistance to local authorities willing to build housing for the poor in buildings and on sites that would be city-owned. Funding was provided as a direct and universal subsidy of $5,000 per unit (equivalent to $94,000 today). This low price frustrated housing advocates of the day and resulted in rather Spartan designs, located on less expensive sites, in unfavorable locations.[165] Nevertheless, tens of thousands of new units were built prior to the outbreak of WWII (many of them close to war production facilities, in anticipation of the coming conflict).

The Techwood Homes project in Atlanta is credited as the first of these projects, completed in 1936. President Roosevelt dedicated it in

Figure 4-6. Techwood housing project Atlanta, Georgia. America's first federally funded low-in-come housing. Shown in late 1930s. Largely demolished 1999. Image: Wikimedia commons.

person. It was built on the cleared site of a mixed-race community de-clared a "slum." While those displaced were both White and Black, only White families were rehoused therein. Assigning housing projects to ei-ther White of Black families was a practice that would officially last until the '60s with a legacy that endures to this day.[166]

Like many such projects, it was unsuccessful as a neighborhood, and was largely demolished in 1996 to be replaced by mixed-use and mixed-income community Centennial Place.

Centennial Place is a first in its own right, credited as the first Hope

---

165   (Radford, 1996)
166   (Gotham, 2000)

VI[167] funded transformation of a publicly owned housing project into a largely privately owned mixed-use, mixed-income community.[168] As with many Hope VI projects, the site was developed with a private corporate partner (The Integral Group LLC) which now owns and manages the site.

It is certainly worth noting that this Hope VI project, like many oth-

Figure 4-7. A typical street in Centennial Place with mixed-income buildings right and Techwood Historic District shown left, with preserved original housing block shown. Towers of Downtown Atlanta shown in distance. Image: Google maps.

ers across the US, returned scarce publicly owned urban land to the private sector, eliminating an available public land opportunity for future use. It's also important to note: according to estimates, less than half of Hope VI project occupants nationwide were rehoused on the revived sites or provided housing vouchers to secure suitable alternative housing nearby.[169] The privatization of public infrastructure, in this case housing, has been a hallmark of the neoliberal and neoclassical '90s-era political economy. While the new mix of incomes, uses, and races is laudable, it raises the question: In these times of glaring inequality and rampant

---

167   Hope VI projects were federally funded initiatives to turn over public housing projects to private sector companies, who would then tear down or alter existing buildings and rebuild the site as a mixed-income privately owned and managed housing complex. Typically, ambitions would include integrating the new project into the fabric of the city in an attempt to blur the previous distinction between the "projects" and the surrounding city.

168   (Turpov, 2005) The longer history of Hope VI includes the seminal work in Boston, where the well-located (near the water) but isolated (from the city) 1950s-era Columbia Point Housing Project was sold off in 1984 (via an open competition) to Corcoran-Mullins-Jennison Developments Co. In its place they built Harbor Point Apartments, a mixed-income community where many, but by no means all, former Columbia Point residents were eventually housed. The privatization of Columbia Point became the model for later Hope VI federal legislation, which passed the US Congress in 1992.

169   (National Housing Law Project; the Poverty & Race Research Action Council; Sherwood Research Associates, and Everywhere and Now Public Housing Residents Organizing Nationally Together, 2002)

home and rent price inflation, is it wise to further reduce public options for housing in this way?

Post-war housing

The turn against the projects

Hundreds of thousands of federally financed public housing units were built after WWII for returning veterans, for the "officially" poor and for elderly Americans of limited means.[170] Nearly all of them employed urban design strategies that departed dramatically from tradition. Gone were the streets and front yards/stoops of virtually all previous American neighborhoods. In their place were parking lots and apartment blocks set in greenswards. Of greatest architectural influence were the ideas of Swiss/French architect Le Corbusier, whose pre-WWII visions for a Radiant City[171] of modernist tower blocks set in verdant parks were enthusiastically taken up by post-war planners and designers. Streets and side-

Figure 4-8. Model of the Plan Voisin for Paris by Le Corbusier displayed at the Nouveau Esprit Pavilion (1925). East Bank of Paris cleared in this unrealized Radiant City plan. Image: Wikimedia Commons.

170   (Hays, 1995)
171   (Corbusier, 1967)

walks were banished from these plans, as were direct connections between streets and buildings.

The "tower in the park" pattern was later criticized by the likes of Jane Jacobs, author of *The Death and Life of Great American Cities*,[172] and Oscar Newman, author of *Defensible Space*,[173] for exhibiting a flawed understanding of how people use and defend city spaces. That failure was made paradigmatic in the notorious Pruitt-Igoe housing project in St. Louis, demolished by its own housing authority only 20 years after construction for irreparable flaws in the basic building and site design.[174]

Figure 4-9. Single loaded corridor at Pruit-Igoe as imagined (left) and prior to demolition (right). Images: U.S. Department of Housing and Urban Development.

This and other failures caused planners, designers, and the public to question, not only the formal strategies used in public housing projects, but also the need for and efficacy of public housing in general.

By the 1980s, the federal government had largely abandoned the mission of housing the poor directly, shifting to providing cash subsidies directly to the individuals for use in the private rental market (discussed below) and providing tax credits to private developers to stimulate low- and moderate-income housing (also discussed below).

Still, it should be noted that these post-war efforts left us with over a million public housing units sheltering 2.1 million Americans.[175] This is less than 1 percent of all Americans, but in some cities the ratio is much higher, notably New York where nearly 5 percent of residents (over 400,000) are publicly housed. [176]

---

172   (Jacobs, 1961)
173   (Newman, 1972)
174   (Chicago : Council of Planning Librarians, 1987) The failure of this project remains controversial. Architects often blame management for its failure, while urbanists blame urban design. It's probably fair to blame both, particularly since other city-managed low-income housing projects, where buildings were more ground oriented and better integrated into the street also failed in many respects, but none failed so spectacularly as Pruitt Igoe.
175   (Boarderless Charity Inc., 2017)
176   (Bloom, 2016)

Figure 4-10. April 1972. The second, widely televised demolition of a Pruitt-Igoe building that followed the March 16 demolition. Image: U.S. Department of Housing and Urban Development.

These numbers are, however, verging on pathetic in comparison to those housed by other western democracies. They provide non-market housing solutions ranging from 17 percent of all units in England[177] to over 50 percent of all housing units in Vienna.[178]

Just give people cash – Section 8 vouchers

Partly due to the problems associated with concentrating the poor in the "projects" and partly due to the fact that by the late '70s the housing problems for poor families had less to do with substandard housing, and more to do with the high cost of acceptable housing, the federal government started to supplement incomes so that the poor could afford market rentals. Currently, 1.1 million Americans receive Section 8 vouchers (named for the section in the housing legislation which enabled them) to help them pay the rent.[179] Vouchers are available to qualified applicants but, because there are far fewer than needed, preference is given to families with children, the aged, and the disabled. Since the amount of the vouchers is tied to "market rents," the federal government becomes one more entity competing for a share of urban land and a player in propping up the asset values thereof.

Tax credits for affordable housing

As the federal government turned away from public housing projects and as a supplement to Section 8 housing vouchers, the United States increased its use of tax credits to spur the construction of low-income housing by the private sector. In simplest terms, tax credits for housing work like this: private development firms are induced to build mixed-income housing in return for tax credits, which could then be sold to high-income individuals or corporations to reduce their annual tax obligations. The credits are capped at a maximum of 70 percent of the total cost of the project. In return, project developers have to partner with a

---

177   (Gov. UK n.d.) It should be noted that in the late '70s over half of all UK citizens lived in "council housing." Margaret Thatcher's government radically increased the "right to buy" program, allowing residents to buy their flat at below-market-rate, moving tens of thousands of units out of the public sector. In time, most of these units ended up in the hands of commercial landlords. (Beckett, 201)

178   (Condon, 2018)

179   (Center on Budget and Policy Priorities, 2019) Section 8 vouchers were intended to allow the poor to rent homes anywhere and thus escape the pathologies of disadvantaged neighborhoods (colloquially called "ghettos"). Critics show that such an escape is rare because rent subsidies are only adequate to rent in the same low-income areas they were supposed to escape. (Semuels, 2015)

local housing agency to find low- and moderate-income households who would pay only 30 percent of their pretax income in rent. After 15 or 30 years (depending on the structure of the deal), the obligation to rent to low- and moderate-income residents would cease and the project would then revert, without further obligation, to the owner. For over 30 years, these public-private partnerships have provided the bulk of new federally subsidized units, providing more than $6 billion per year in tax credits to produce more than 50,000 units per year annually (or about $12,000 per unit).[180] The program has been criticized for costing, on average, 30 percent more per unit than similar private market projects, along with associated fraud.[181] As is the case for rental vouchers (described above), this is, in essence, taxpayer money (in the form of taxes never received [credits] and a consequent shift of federal costs to other taxpayers) funneled to private hands, who then purchase urban land. It is yet another tax-funded competitor in the limited market for suitable housing land and a contributor to skyrocketing urban land Rent.

Mortgage interest deductions

Of possibly more subtle, but even greater influence on urban land markets are those federal inducements for Americans to enter the housing market and become homeowners. Prior to the 2008 Great Recession, nearly 69 percent of all Americans lived in a home owned by family member(s).[182] The crash was caused by the transformation of mortgages into an investment commodity, packaged and sold as "mortgage-backed securities" on global capital markets. Purchasers of mortgage-backed securities believed they were shielded from risk, reassured by falsified triple A credit ratings provided by complicit rating agencies (it's a long story).[183]

The home-ownership rate dropped back to 65 percent after the crash, a rate not seen since the '60s. A disproportionate share of that drop was attributable to mortgage defaults by Black mortgagees, erasing modest

---

180   (Volker, 2010)
181   (Stamm, 2020)
182   (Hueble, 2019)
183   (Lewis, 2011) Later made into a feature-length movie, The Big Short illustrates, among other things, the degree of complicity on the part of ratings agencies such as Moody's. Moody's and other rating agencies ignored the risk of mortgage-backed securities, which would fail if the housing market began to slide. And slide it did. Wall Street banks failed and global finance froze, at huge eventual cost to taxpayers. Only a few "short sellers" saw it coming, and bet against these securities (by taking out insurance on securities they didn't even own). When those securities failed, they made billions. At the time of this writing, Carl Icahn made a similar killing by shorting securities backing shopping malls that failed during the 2020 pandemic. (Kelly, 2020)

wealth gains of the 1980s and 1990's.

The housing market and the economy

The strength of the American economy is tied to the housing market. The housing market accounts for up to 18 percent of annual GDP and represents 71 percent of household debt held by Americans[184] (really by banks since the bank technically owns the house until the very last payment on the loan).

The mortgage interest rate deduction primarily benefits Americans in the upper quartile of income and amounts to a huge annual loss in federal taxes (up until 2017, annual taxes forgone due to this deduction were in the range of $60 billion annually, 10 times more than is lost to the low-income housing credits discussed above).[185] Most economists suggest it doesn't actually make housing more affordable either.[186] Why? Because its value gets absorbed in higher housing prices or in the form of excessively sprawling suburban development, with the main beneficiaries being (you guessed it) land speculators. Evidence to support this contention is found by comparing home ownership rates in Canada, where there are no mortgage interest rate deductions, and the US, where there are. Home ownership rates are almost identical to US rates, while the average density of Canadian cities is substantially higher.[187]

Conclusion

It is now estimated that between all the various government initiatives listed above, less than a third of qualified Americans enjoy federal housing supports. As American inequality rages, increasingly manifest in the ever-widening gap between average wages and average housing costs, particularly in jobs-rich coastal cities, this number is shrinking further. Federal and state governments are not increasing and, by many measures are decreasing, housing assistance in response.[188]

Also important to bear in mind, in the entire history of publicly

---

184   (Fontinelle, 2019)
185   It is now $25 billion, down from $60 billion as of 2017 as a result of the Tax Cuts and Jobs Act of 2017. In the context of that bill it's hard to celebrate this change since it merely helped pay for a small portion of the loss in taxes due to tax cuts for rich Americans passed in the same bill. The elimination of the deduction applied only to homes over $500,000 in value, which hit high-housing-cost coastal cities the hardest.
186   (Casselman, 2015)
187   Los Angeles is the exception to the rule. Figures for Vancouver are skewed by inclusion of substantial green zone within the boundaries of "urbanized area." (Demographia, 2000)
188   (Rice, 2016)

assisted housing efforts, American governments have not found a way to mitigate the ever-increasing cost of urban land. On the contrary, from the Depression era to today, government actors have been one more competitor in the market for increasingly limited urban lands, doing their part to bid up prices. Unlike other nations, the US has never seriously entertained the notion that land values are a consequence of community actions over time and that at least some of that benefit should escape the grip of land speculators. As shown in Chapters one and two, the victims of this political economy are largely the Black and the Brown and the young. The result is not simply economic deprivation, but health inequity as well. The Black, the Brown, and increasingly the young are now up to four times more likely to become ill and die from communicable diseases like COVID-19. This certainly suggests that "building back better" should go beyond the usual paean for "highways, roads and bridges" – all to serve an urban landscape of ever greater inequality – but should rather be a call to engineer an urban landscape where we better manage our land resource for more equitable and healthy national outcomes. Streaming land Rents to finance affordable housing is the most obvious and easiest way to accomplish this goal.

Chapter 5

The Vienna model and the 21st century American city

Introduction

G iven the gravity of the systemic and linked crises explored in this volume, it is wise to look for successful models from other lands that the US might emulate. Sadly, after 40 years of neoliberal inspired privatizations, there are very few global cities one can look to for equitable housing models that easily map over the form, economics, and culture of American cities. Singapore is often mentioned as an attractive model, but the land of that city, and thus its Rents, are largely in public hands. Somehow, moving trillions of dollars' worth of vested interests in American urban land to public hands seems unlikely in the extreme.

The Netherlands is often mentioned in the same breath as Sweden; where dramatic increases in publicly owned housing occurred in the immediate post-WWII period of Social Democrat-inspired housing production. But there, too, more recent neoliberal enthusiasm for market-based approaches have led to a net decline in the proportion of citizens protected from insecure housing and a corresponding rise in land Rents.

Germany, and Berlin especially, was until just a few years ago touted as a model. There, most residents are renters, living in medium-density urban blocks, presumably protected by unique housing laws. But recent staggering shifts of housing stock to international real-estate investment trusts and associated 50 percent rises in rents have provoked angry street demonstrations, with citizens there demanding the return to public hands of hundreds of housing blocks sold off during their late 20th-century privatization binge.[189]

So while it is depressing to admit it, and while it does not bode well for our future efforts, there is truly only one advanced city that has solved the housing equity problem and provides a suitable model for the 21st-century US: Vienna.

Figure 5-1. The strongly set back central wing with its six monumental towers of the listed residential complex Karl-Marx-Hof of the municipality of Vienna in the 19th district of Döbling. The building with 1382 (currently around 1270) residential units was built from 1927--1933 according to plans by the architect Karl Ehn (the official opening of the facility took place on October 12, 1930). It is probably not the most representative, but certainly the best-known communal residential building in the city of Vienna. As a prime example of a monumental residential super block, it extends over 1,100 meters along Heiligenstädter Strasse, making it the longest contiguous residential building in the world. Image: Wikimedia Commons.

The Vienna model - history

Vienna, during the last days of the Hapsburgs, demonstrated its wealth in the form of impressive building facades. But behind the façade was a grimmer reality. Workers were crowded 10 to a 300 sq. ft. flat. Many slept four to a bed. Some workers used their beds in shifts, hiring out sleeping space during the day, while the principal tenant was at work – all to pay

---

189   (Reuters, 2019)

the usurious rents. Are we heading this way again?

This Vienna was a city run by and for the landlords, wealthy owners of lands that had once been farms but that now sprouted apartment buildings. Males of wealth, most of them landlords, were the only residents who could vote. Thus, in a city that at the dawn of WWI contained over two million residents, less than 60,000 could vote. With control over public policy so heavily tipped to landlords, renters had no protection. One-month leases were common and rents could be raised at any time with no recourse for tenants. Evictions were immediate, without cause and without adjudication.

The gravity of this housing crisis, and the plight of the people, can be measured by the number of the homeless. In 1913 there were 461,472 people living in asylums (homeless shelters by another name), an astonishing quarter of the population. About 29,000 of these homeless were children. [190]

When Austria and its allies were defeated in the First World War, the Hapsburg monarchy collapsed. Universal suffrage followed and voting rights, previously extended to only two percent of the population, were now granted to all, regardless of income or gender. This precipitated a dramatic leftward shift in Vienna's politics, but in an unusual form.

The First World War was unkind to both victors and vanquished, destabilizing democracies and monarchies alike. The rise of Hitler, and the 75-year reign by Russian communists are the most well-known consequences; but many other governments, democracies and monarchies alike, were similarly destabilized.

For the next generation, citizens throughout Europe separated themselves into political camps ranging from Marxist internationalists on the far left to fascist nationalists on the far right, unleashing inevitable internal conflicts and the eventual conflagration of the Second World War. Austria's political trajectory was somewhat different – but only at first.

With the fall of the Austro-Hungarian Empire, and with the universal suffrage that this collapse made possible, the political left gained power that it retained until the Depression and the rise of Italian and German fascism precipitated a right-wing takeover in 1934. The relatively short period between 1917 and 1934 is called the "Red Vienna" period, for the socialist leanings of its city leaders.

Significantly, elected and appointed officials during the Red Vienna

---

190   (Reiss, 2017) Much of this history is distilled from Reiss's study.

Figure 5-2. Anton-Schmid-Hof Public housing, Construction: 1964-1966. Architects: Egon Fraundorfer, Robert Kotas, Eugenie Pippal-Kottnig, & Rudolf Hönig. Image: Wikimedia Commons.

period, unlike leftist parties in other parts of Europe – never set out to remove or even cripple capitalism by nationalizing property. Instead they used a taxing strategy to meet their social ends – and their most important end was providing decent housing for every resident. In this they succeeded. How?

The financing

A number of regulatory and taxing policies made Vienna's housing system possible. Even before the Red Vienna period, a key policy was imposed that was crucial to the city's later success: strict rent control. The government had imposed it to prevent war wives from being evicted while their husbands fought at the front. It was never repealed. The government outlawed raising rents beyond a minimal amount and, in the presence of extreme currency inflation, made it less profitable to build new rental stock.[191]

Ordinarily this would be a very bad thing for affordability, as rental stock is usually less expensive per month (in the short-term at least) than home ownership. Thus, policies that impede the construction of rental

---

191   The private rental market remains viable, just not usurious. Rate of return is 3 to 4 percent rather than the 10 percent common in other countries. Apartments rent for about 25 percent of price for similar Paris apartments. New private apartments still get built and are economically viable because rent control laws keep land prices low. (Tirone, 2006)

housing are generally frowned upon. This is true in many US cities today, where officials often go to great lengths to induce the private market to produce new rental stock through subsidy, relaxed taxes, or density bonuses. But sadly, the monthly rents charged for these new market-rate units are typically unaffordable for all but the upper tier of renters. This same problem is a feature of housing markets in other unaffordable cities throughout the developed world.

Vienna provides an interesting counterpoint. Because rent control disincentivized the private development of rental buildings, landlords were, for a time, removed from the market for urban land. Consequently, prices for development land went down, allowing the city to buy land at a much reduced price; often the city was the only buyer in the market. The reduced price was the consequence of falling land Rents – land Rents lowered by the imposition of rent control. Rent control in this case advantageously limited the flow of labor and capital value into land Rents.

Given Vienna's newly powerful position in the land market, the city quickly became the dominant developer of new residential projects. Vienna had the wisdom to retain the city's best architects and developers to design and build this new housing, employing skills honed in service to the private sector to now build public-sector housing. [192]

Figure 5-3. Somogyi-Hof at Hütteldorfer Straße 150-158 in Vienna's XIV district. Designed by the architects Heinrich Schmid and Hermann Aichinger in 1927 for the city of Vienna as communal housing. Named after the socialist writer Béla Somogyi (1868-1920). Image: Gryffindor, Wikimedia Commons.

---

192   (Förster, 2016) Much of this overview of contemporary practices comes from *The Vienna Model : Housing for the Twenty-First-Century City.*

A fifth of this new housing was "social housing," intended for the poor and disabled. But the bulk of the new housing was for wage earners and their families, to be owned and managed by co-operatives or nonprofit housing corporations. Vienna's nonprofit housing corporations operate just like for-profit housing corporations, except that their profits are poured back into operations, and their continued operations are governed by city contracts controlling, among other things, the amount of rent to be asked of tenants. Now about 25 percent of the city's residents live in publicly owned social housing and another 18 percent live in homes owned cooperatively.

Building buildings

Even though the city was able to keep land prices down, land and construction still costs money. In the late 1920s, approximately 30 percent of Vienna's annual budget was spent buying land and financing housing construction. Where did the money come from? Mostly from taxes on private property and land. They were levied on apartment buildings and progressively increased with the assessed value of each unit. Very high taxes were also levied on vacant land, giving owners additional incentive to sell. Their methods were clearly in keeping with methods Henry George had advanced two decades earlier.[193]

What is interesting here is how these policy actions stripped land speculation (and out-of-control Rent) out of the marketplace. Doubtless, any attempt to replicate this strategy in the US, where faith in the "free market" remains strong, would provoke debate. But the gravity of the crisis that Vienna faced and the efficacy of its solution is beyond debate. The situation in jobs-rich coastal US cities is now nearly as grave.

Rent control and Rent

As the housing crisis accelerates, many North American cities are strengthening rent control legislation. Five US states[194] have rent control

---

193   Henry George has more than one connection to Vienna between the wars, most notably with Silvio Gesell (1862-1930), German reformer. In Gesell's main work, The Natural Economic Order through Free Land and Free Money, Gesell opposed the association of "blood" with "land," which of course was the driving ethos of Nazism. Inspired by Henry George and his "Single Tax" on land value, Gesell called upon government to buy land and lease it to the highest bidder and to forgo taxation. A Georgist land tax was attempted in Hungary and Albert Einstein living in Switzerland at the time considered George brilliant: "Men like Henry George are rare, unfortunately. One cannot imagine a more beautiful combination of intellectual keenness, artistic form, and fervent love of justice." (The School of Cooperative Individualism. n.d.)

194   California, Oregon, New York, New Jersey, Maryland.

legislation, while Oregon passed a law in 2019 making rent control the law statewide. Controlling rents is a crucial way to, not only protect tenants, but to also quell the appetite of international real-estate investment trusts (REITs) for a city's land.

Figure 5-4. The Holy-Hof in Hernals, Vienna, public housing project constructed by Rudolf Perco in 1928-1929. Image: Wikimedia Commons.

In Vienna, taxes supporting housing were broadly distributed, including a portion of income taxes now dedicated to housing. Resident Viennese supported these taxes because they received secure housing in return, housing that is much more affordable than homes in most of the world's tier-one cities. Rents in Vienna are less than half that of similar units in Paris.

The state of the Vienna housing market today

However, it is wise to avoid donning rose-colored glasses when considering the Vienna model. Austria has not been entirely immune to the late 20th-century neoliberal enthusiasm for privatization of housing. Nor are the Viennese entirely immune to the attractions of profit-taking in the housing market. Vienna, like many other western democracies, essentially stopped building social housing for the poor by the early 2000s. Laws were changed to allow for the conversion of rental housing into condominiums in the '90s. In the same decade, a "rent to buy" program was introduced in Vienna for new subsidized rental units; they could be purchased by residents after 10 years of occupancy. Rent control laws that governed all apartments built before 1945 were relaxed to let rents float closer to market rents. These shifts have altered the proportion of Viennese housed by tenure, with the biggest shift evident in the rate of home ownership, from 16 percent of all housing to 21 percent in only seven years.[195] Yet despite these shifts, Vienna still builds far more co-operative nonprofit housing each year than any other European county. This increase in market share for market ownership can also be read as a positive shift, since the price of home ownership in Vienna is much closer to average wages than in other European first-tier cities. Why? Because the dominance of the protected housing market, where over 65 percent of residents are still shielded from housing precarity (pre-1945 rent-controlled apartments, 26 percent; social housing for the poor, 24 percent; co-op housing, 18 percent) keeps market land Rents low. With this much urban land protected from Rents, the tendency for private-market lands to inflate up to the maximum levels experienced in New York and other US tier -one cities is mitigated. The Vienna example suggests a balance between a private market for urban land and a protected one is possible and beneficial for both sectors. While housing advocates in Vienna are fearful[196] about these trends, Americans should be so lucky.

Figure 5-5. The semi-detached house Jagdschloßgasse 80, 82 of the Werkbundsiedlung Vienna in the 13th district of Hietzing. Semi-detached house built around 1930 according to plans by the architect Arthur Grünberger. It is part of a model estate of around 70 houses with around 50 different house types that were built between 1929 and 1932. More than 30 architects took part in the planning of the individual houses. Image: Bwag, Wikimedia Commons.

The design process

Vienna also developed a system for working with nonprofit development

---

195   (Gutheil-Knopp-Kirchwald, 2017)
196   (lPrager, 2018)

corporations that compete with each other for the next city-sponsored project. The city acquires the land for a project, establishes the housing goals, and publishes the amount of any financial subsidy to be supplied. Stakeholder groups judge the proposals submitted in response and decide which project team of architect, builder, developer, and management entity has the most intelligent response.

This competitive process ensures that projects are distinctive and varied, a dramatic departure from the process for building public housing in many other countries, where mediocrity would seem to be the goal.

What can US cities learn from the Vienna example?

First, Vienna treats land like the precious public asset that it is. American policy makers, like their earlier Viennese counterparts, can support efforts to acquire and keep land in the hands of the people who live on it. Given migration, demographic, and economic trends, it would seem crucial for US cities to purchase more land on behalf of non-governmental housing providers, whether they be churches, co-ops or charitable organizations. However, cities should, like Vienna, tie land acquisition strategies to policies that reduce Rent, like rent control or affordable housing overlay zones (discussed in the next Chapter). Without these coordinated strategies, cities run the risk of being just one more competitor in the already overheated market for urban land.

Second, when confronted with situations where the majority of their citizens could not find affordable homes, at least one Western capitalist city has solved the problem.

Third, building housing for just the very poor, and leaving wage earners to the maelstrom of the housing market, will erode political support for government intervention and only increase the damaging effect of Rents over time.

Conclusion

There is one more thing to mention. Viennese pay co-op rents that are not tied to income level. These rents cover the cost of upkeep and replacement but do not repay the original city subsidies. Thus, their rental rates are far below 30 percent of average tenant income. In return for this cost break, citizens seem willing to pay housing taxes to support this housing system. These low rental rates are now part of the tradition of the city and unlikely to change without political disruption.

However, for US cities this choice has yet to be made. If we assume that any city can manage to quell the fierce inflation in land cost through some combination of land use controls, rent controls, and/or taxing policy, and if we assume that a local economy will produce enough middle-class jobs such that renters have money to pay, there is no reason that non-market housing can't eventually fully repay land and construction costs to the city.

Figure 5-6. Hundertwasser housing complex. Corner of Kegelgasse / Löwengasse of the Hundertwasserhaus in Vienna's 3rd district, Landstrasse. The residential complex of the municipality of Vienna with 50 residential units was built as an eco-house from 1983 to 1985. It was designed by the artist Friedensreich Hundertwasser, in collaboration with architects Josef Krawina and Peter Pelikan. Image: Bwag, Wikimedia.

After an initial period of subsidy, it is conceivable that, through intelligent management of policy and taxing levers, public coffers need not be constantly drained to provide non-market housing for the majority of wage earners. A system can be built that would, over time, return to the city all the money supplied. Construction costs are not the problem, the problem is the price of land. If through public policy land prices can be reined in, then broad-based housing affordability can be achieved, without the need for perpetual subsidy.

Chapter 6

Policy solutions

Introduction

Many have tried to solve the American housing affordability problem – and all have failed – at no time failing as spectacularly as in recent decades. Having abandoned any pretense of providing new public housing, and with ever-decreasing state and federal housing assistance funding on offer, these decades stand out as remarkably weak, particularly during a time when precarious housing has become a fact of life for an ever-increasing share of the American population.

Furthermore, what taxpayer money has been spent on affordable housing has been largely directed towards private housing providers, ultimately adding that much more fuel to the raging dumpster fire of land price inflation. Given that the pandemic has shown that the vector for disease is inequality, and thus that protecting the health of Americans is now added to the ongoing task of eliminating racial and economic injustice from our shores, political support is clearly increasing for practical and implementable urban development solutions that do more than funnel yet more taxpayer funds into private hands as Rent. And appropriately, these new solutions are being initiated at the local level where housing actually gets built. Examples of important first steps in this direction are outlined in this Chapter. But first to recap.

Our problem and its causes, as articulated in previous Chapters, is recapitulated below:

1. The vector for disease is not density, not transportation, and only partly barriers to affordable health care. The vector is geographic inequality. Vulnerable populations are sorted by race and class into the same neighborhoods – sorted almost entirely by housing cost – subject to both contagion and spread of disease in their crowded homes, their local cafés, and in the service industries where they work.

2. Laudable attempts to increase affordability by increasing allowable density have not made homes more affordable; they have primarily enriched land speculators.

3. The vigor of both capital and labor is inordinately absorbed by urban land Rents, with little tangible benefit to anyone other than, yet again, the land speculator.

4. Our present circumstances are largely unprecedented: Never in our short national history has our urban land been so thoroughly globalized, financialized, and hoarded. And never in the past 80 years has the gap between hourly wages and the cost of housing been so great.

Housing policy and American politics

Before turning to explore practical policy solutions, it is wise to restate a few obvious truths. It's axiomatic that for solutions to succeed they must be politically viable. The failure of the "Single Tax Movement" provides a useful reminder. Henry George promoted the single tax on land as a means of solving the very same problems described in this volume. Yet after his death, the movement he started failed politically and is virtually unknown today. Why? It fell victim to a pincher movement between both the political left and right.

Those on the political right used their financial power to establish and finance an industry of academic economists hired specifically to argue that land was capital and capital was land – all at the behest of the land barons.[197] Thus was the special toxicity of land Rent rendered invisible. We still live under their spell.

Those on the left, the socialists of his day, argued that Henry George did not go far enough: It was not enough to find clever strategies to treat the pathologies of urban capitalism. Those pathologies had to be excised root and branch. All land had to be nationalized. Nothing less would do,

---

197 (Gaffney, 1993)

they said.[198]

While the principles George espoused remain valid, the biases of both the left and the right are also still in place.

So even though geographic inequality is unsustainable, it is only sensible for housing advocates and policy makers to pursue politically viable (and hopefully consensus-based) strategies as correctives. Thus, it makes sense, both as a practical and as a political matter, for policy makers to leave the basic structure of real-estate economy in place, while turning as much land Rent to social purpose as possible.

Henry George wrote eloquently on the special suitability of a tax on Rents for the American cultural context. His arguments are still true today. America is not a place where collective ownership of the means of production (or land) will gain public support. But neither is it a place where citizens believe that landlords should have the same power as the British landed classes, against whom they revolted. The Chapter that follows describes strategies that successfully balance these tendencies, strategies grounded in already constitutionally approved and successfully implemented urban development practices.

The influence of housing policy on land speculation

As the word "speculation" connotes, urban land is speculated on in anticipation of future gains. That begs the question: can we use development policy to influence that expectation? The answer is of course we can. We do it all the time, typically in two ways, as follows:

1. Sometimes we choose to limit new urban construction. When we do that we freeze available supply and boost land prices, and stimulate speculation.

2. Sometimes we choose to boost new housing construction. When we do that we signal investment opportunity. And again we boost land prices and stimulate speculation.

Thus, very oddly, it seems that either freezing or expanding housing supply increases the cost of homes. The idea that limiting supply increases prices is an idea that appeals to our common sense. But it is also true that boosting allowable density to increase housing supply inflates land

---

198   (Miller, 2000)

prices such that hoped for affordability gains are lost.[199] How then can we use policy to benefit future homeowners and renters rather than land speculators?

Certain municipal level taxes and development controls have proven to be effective remedies for the problem. Of these, the property tax is the best known.

Changing municipal tax rates on land

Municipal taxes on land already exist and can be used to lower land Rents. Unlike national and state governments, American municipalities have typically depended on property taxes to fund public services. All but one state, Oklahoma,[200] have authorized their cities to levy property taxes on real estate. Most states also demand that municipalities not tax property beyond a certain rate (a trend begun in 1978 when California voters passed "Proposition 13," [201] which limited residential property taxes to no more than 1 percent of value annually).[202] As property values have exploded in recent years, and as states have been slow to lower these thresholds, property tax caps based on market value have become less fiscally confining. However, the lack of public appetite for new taxes makes it politically difficult to levy steep new taxes on land in the way that Henry George favored. Nevertheless, it's worth understanding how Henry George's land tax ideas might influence American urban development, and how, in some cases, they already have.

To operate in a way that eliminated Rents, as George proposed, the full value of a parcel of land should be taxed. Not paid all at once but in instalments like a mortgage: i.e. a land tax of 7 percent to 9 percent of the land's estimated total Rent value each year. This sounds harsh, but in practice, if land taxes were this high, homeowners (and renters) would not spend more per month on housing. This is because the purchase price for the land itself would be driven down close to zero by the tax liability. Thus the purchase price for a home would not be based on land value,

---

199   This is a contentious point and, as argued earlier, defies the so called "law of supply and demand." It seems counterintuitive that increasing supply increases cost until you view it through the lens of land Rents. As cities add intensity, the value of new economic activities does not go to workers or entrepreneurs, but gets absorbed in land Rents (or in commonplace terms, in the form of land price inflation). Thus a new high-rise not only correlates with much increased site land value but helps inflate the land Rents of surrounding parcels as well. Ahlfeldt and Pietrostefani (Ahlfeldt, 2017) provide an exhaustive compilation of the evidence to support this view.

200   (Urban Institute, 2011)

201   (Wikipedia n.d.)

202   (Californias law also limits annual increases to no more than 2 percent, particularly problematic during times of high inflation. However this constraint lapses when the property is sold.)

but on the replacement cost of the improvements (structures). Finally, the value of the structures would not be taxed at all.

Taxing just land would also have the salutary effect of favoring home types that are more efficient users of land, for example, placing fourplexes on a single parcel rather than a single-family home. True, the amount of land value equity built up by a homeowner over the course of a mortgage would also be zero. Only the building would accrue equity in this case. But this, too, provides homeowners with a strong rationale for improving the structure(s) on the land, (rather than depending primarily on land value increases to build personal wealth).

Twenty-nine US states assess property in a way that distinguishes land value from the value of improvements,[203] a clear legacy of the impact of Henry George. However, most states tend to use the same tax rate (called a mil rate) for both the structure and the land. Inspired by the single tax argument, the State of Pennsylvania authorizes its municipalities to tax urban land and improvements at different rates if they so choose. A number of Pennsylvania cities have used differential tax rates on land to avoid disinvestments in their older districts consequent to urban sprawl[204] – disinvestments that still plague many other rust-belt cities of a similar size. Harrisburg, Pennsylvania is a case in point.

By the 1980s, Harrisburg, a medium-sized city and the state capital, was faced with Detroit-level property declines and abandonment. The city responded by shifting taxes away from improvements onto land. Now land is taxed at five times the rate of improvements. When the city

Figure 6-1. Traditional downtown street in Harrisburg, PA. Property conditions stabilized through use of disproportional tax on land at five times the rate of improvement. Image: Google Maps.

---

203   (M. E. Bell, 2006)
204   High land taxes favor denser development, where land parcels are small and buildings large. This favors older more traditional parts of cities characterized by small lots and tight urban blocks, and disincentivizes sprawling large-lot subdivisions.

made that change, 90 percent of residential properties in the older, denser parts of the city saw their tax bill go down, shoring up the value of easier to service smaller, older, urban lots.

The city had 4,200 abandoned structures in 1985. By 2001, a decade and a half after shifting taxes to land, it had only 500. City coffers, near bankruptcy in the 1980s, by 2000 were in balance again, and legacy infrastructure (which had been wasting away) could be maintained anew. [205]

Policy makers in states where differential rates on land and improvements are allowed should consider adding this tool to their housing affordability tool-box. If states restrict this option, it would be a no-cost change worth proposing. If Harrisburg is any guide, it helps prevent the decay of older neighborhoods.

More important, but politically more difficult, might be to adjust land rates with the specific intention of driving land prices down, while producing revenue to support non-market housing options in one's city. Viewed as pure policy, this is an effective way to drive down land Rents and fund non-market housing at the same time, with only the land speculators left worse off. Finally, policy makers at the municipal level seldom recognize that, given their control of land development policy and property tax, they are the only level of government that can control land Rents. Thus, they have far more power to alter geographic inequality than do state or federal officials. And property taxes are not their only tool. They also control zoning approvals and development taxes that can be used to the same effect, as discussed below.

Exactions and bonuses for affordable housing.

Generally, there are two types of public-policy tools used widely to secure affordable housing: exactions and bonuses. Exactions are basically a tax on development with funds used to secure non-market housing units. Bonuses are approvals for additional saleable value beyond "as of right" limits in return for non-market housing units. "As of right" refers to a zoning limit already stipulated in ordinances. Giving bonuses is a special permitting process that grants more intense land use than an ordinance authorizes in return for a negotiated number of non-market housing units.

These basic strategies have survived constitutional challenges many times. Cities have well-established powers to use zoning to limit

---

205   (Vincent, 2019)

private-property rights to protect the "health, safety, and welfare" of the general population. Supreme Court challenges dating back 100 years support this.[206] More recent court cases specific to affordable housing requirements have reinforced this public right (although challenges continue to come before the high court, as recently as 2019).[207] City officials are thus not obligated to ensure "highest and best use" (meaning maximum possible profits) for privately held parcels, if a health, safety, and welfare basis can be established. In terms Henry George might use, cities are not required to ensure that the owners of development parcels must be rewarded, to the penny, for the value of improvements made by citizens on lands that surround their parcel. This is no small thing. This limit on property rights provides policy makers with a tool to ensure that social benefits accrue from the urban development they authorize. This power is already widely used, just at a scale that only weakly influences land Rents.

Exactions and the approval process

Negotiating exactions on a project-by-project basis is particularly unsettling for proponents, as project pro formas and "residual" land value calculations are difficult to ensure in such circumstances. Developers may have already purchased or "optioned"[208] development parcels years in advance based on predictions of what will be exacted. And since land must be secured well in advance of permit approvals, a faulty guess can be very costly. This likely explains why many American municipalities have been too timid to admit that driving down land price might be the point. The pages that follow offer a representative sampling of policy strategies now in use to exact affordable housing units in return for incentives to developers (instead of taxpayer subsidies, as in public housing projects, previously described). All of these policy strategies can be viewed through a Georgist lens as a means to stream wealth that would have otherwise increased land Rents (enriching only land speculators) into permanently affordable housing.

---

206   (Simpson, 1969)

207   The high court chose to return a 2019 case to lower courts without finding, letting stand the affirmative decision by that court in the case of Dartmond Cherk v. Marin County (Boerne, 2020).

208   "Options" in real estate are agreements between a developer and a landowner wherein the landowner offers a developer an "option" to purchase the land at a fixed price at some future date. If a developer is successful in getting bank financing and planning approval s/he can "exercise the option" and buy the land at the previously agreed price. If not, the option is not exercised and the landowner can sell to another person.

Impact fees

The most common form of exaction, and the one most widely used, is the "impact fee," a fee imposed when parcels are rezoned for a more intensive (and lucrative) use. Impact fees are still most commonly used to pay for off-site infrastructure (upgrading a sewer interceptor or re-signalizing a nearby traffic intersection, for example), but are increasingly used to fund affordable housing. Impact fees for affordable housing (used in California, New Jersey, Massachusetts, Colorado and Florida) are typically levied at modest levels. But there is no court finding standing in the way of requiring fees (coincident with, say, a tripling of allowable density) at a level adequate to produce one permanently affordable unit for every market-rate unit in a proposed project should nexus studies support this rate.

California's municipalities, likely because of the severity of its housing crisis, have been less timid than most states in imposing affordable housing impact fees. More than 16 California cities have used impact fees to fund affordable housing directly; impact fees that must necessarily shift value from land Rent to public purpose. As would be expected, landowners have challenged these cash exactions on more than one occasion. California and US courts have responded by allowing fees for affordable housing if a "nexus" study is performed to show that a project will generate an identifiable need for affordable housing.[209] Municipalities have successfully shown that the production of market-rate housing will produce a need for homes for low- and moderate-wage service providers in some proportion to high-wage earners, and that requiring the production of same is a proper use of "police power." At the time of this writing, the nexus studies have provided evidence that market-rate housing projects generate a need for affordable units, at a typical ratio of one unit affordable to every three market-rate units.[210] As housing inequality becomes more extreme, with housing costs for wage earners more and more out of reach, it follows that newer nexus studies will show an increasing need for affordable units, likely in the range of 1 to 2 or even 1 to 1. This would mitigate the tendency for land prices to inflate in proportion to new density allowances, and thus redirect land value increases toward socially crucial ends.

Approximately 60 percent of US cities with more than 25,000

---

209   (Preiss, 2017)
210   (Keyser Marston Associates, Inc. 2016) Example is from Albany California.

residents now impose impact fees to fund the infrastructure needed to service new housing.[211] A far smaller number currently impose impact fees to fund affordable housing. In California, affordable housing impact fees were added to fees for off-site infrastructure relatively recently, partly in response to a court case that limited inclusionary zoning policies in that state.[212]

An informal analysis by the Non-Profit Housing Association of Northern California found that among Bay Area jurisdictions that replaced inclusionary zoning policies with affordable housing impact fees, all of the adopted impact fees were less than the "cash in-lieu" fees of their prior inclusionary zoning program. While the in-lieu fees had been based on the cost of providing an affordable housing unit, the impact fees were based on a nexus study. Most cities chose to set their impact fee well below the maximum fee suggested by their nexus studies.

Do exactions add to home price?

Evidence indicates that, over the long-term,[213] final sale prices to new home purchasers are not elevated by imposed development fees, as final home purchase prices are set by the strength of the regional housing market and the advantages provided to residents by city living. The fee levels ultimately affect and reduce the "residual" value of land. This is because the upside price limit for new homes (usually based on price per interior square foot) is capped by city and region-wide housing market strength. Development taxes imposed on a single parcel or zone will not change that. However, a development tax imposed late in the approval process may make the business case for a project unworkable. At that point, the project will either be canceled or the price for the land will be renegotiated down. Municipalities are therefore in a position to moderate or eliminate land price inflation by signaling their intention to impose a development tax years ahead of time. One might call this process "disciplining the land market."

The point to emphasize here is that municipalities are the most

---

211 (GAO, 2000)
212 (Grounded Solutions, 2019)
213 The question "do impact fees raise home prices, yes or no?" is contentious still. The common-sense reaction is "Of course they do! Fees add cost!" To make matters worse, studies give different results based on methodology and duration of study. The most exhaustive study, a meta-analysis from 2005 (Been, 2005) showed that market prices increased in the short-term but equalized in the long-term as the land markets and developers adjusted to new costs. This conforms to the hypothesis of this text: ergo, that land taxes, if clearly known in advance by the "market," do not increase house prices but rather lower land cost.

powerful and in most states the only, level of government that can control
the speculative value of urban land with the stroke of a pen. Insisting that
financial exactions drawn from project proponents be used for affordable
housing has been ruled legitimate use of police power by courts. It is
thus both legal and increasingly necessary to use these policy and taxing
tools to drive down land Rents and to increase affordable housing at the
same time. To understand this a bit better, it's worth learning about what
developers call "residual value."

Residual value

Purchase prices for development parcels are determined by the "residual
value" (land value that remains)[214] after all costs of construction, profits,
and fees are deducted from expected total sales price. Residual value can
be thought of as the "left over" amount you can offer a landowner after
expenses, and drops as development costs elevate. Development fees are
part of that list of expenses. As development fees go up, land prices go
down. Theoretically, municipalities can elevate fees to the point where
land prices drop to zero. This would, again in theory, reduce land Rents
to zero as Henry George would recommend. But exactions equal to or
just below the "land lift" value increase consequent to a higher density
authorization will dampen the tendency for land prices to inflate, leaving
original land prices unaffected by proposed new area or city plans and/or
project approvals. In jobs-rich coastal cities, where land Rents are already
far out of control, it would be more than sensible to calibrate a suite of
exactions and bonuses that would have kept land Rents stable as the goal.
It would even be appropriate to use these policies to nudge land prices
lower over time.

Henry George did not propose these strategies. Why?

During his short life, Henry George did not propose zoning policies and
development taxes as a potential solution to the problem of urban land
Rents because, when he wrote *Progress and Poverty*, zoning ordinances
and development fees did not exist. The US did not even have a national
income or business tax at that time, but depended almost entirely on
duties and excise taxes to finance the federal budget. A federal income
tax would not become a fact of life until the late 1910s and zoning would

---

214   (Property Metrics, 2019)

not pass constitutional muster until 1926.[215] Yet during George's life, the tenuous status of the US on the world stage, and the global trend of other nations to concentrate power at federal level, forced the US to find a more robust source of federal tax dollars. It was in this context that George proposed his national land tax. After his death and after two decades of debate in Congress, the nation chose to pursue a national income tax (in 1909) rather than a national land value tax (much to the dismay of Henry George Jr., Henry George's son, who was serving in Congress at the time). [216]

Inclusive zoning requirements

Inclusive zoning refers to programs or policies that require or incentivize the creation of affordable housing for new development. Inclusionary zoning ordinances have not been shown to increase prices of market units in the same project, but rather to lower prices of developable parcels.[217]

A 2016 Lincoln Institute for Land Policy study identified 886 US jurisdictions with inclusionary housing programs located in 25 states in the US and the District of Columbia. About 80 percent of all municipally administered inclusive housing programs are located in just three states: New Jersey (45 percent), Massachusetts (27 percent), and California (17 percent).[218] These states have either state incentives for local policy adoption or state-wide inclusionary housing policies. A total of 1,379 policies were found in 791 jurisdictions. The study identified that 373 jurisdictions reported creating a total of 173,707 units of affordable housing (since inception) and an additional amount of $1.7 billion in impact or in-lieu fees for the creation of affordable housing. This is a laudable achievement but it's worth remembering that the true affordable housing need nationwide is in the many hundreds of billion dollar range.

---

215   *In Village of Euclid vs Ambler Realty Company*, US Supreme Court 1926, Ambler Realty argued that the designation of a client parcel for housing when the parcel was more valuable as industrial land constituted an uncompensated taking. The court, in the end, decided against Ambler, arguing that zoning was a rational extension of "police power," and, if used rationally in pursuit of "health, safety, and welfare," was constitutional (Simpson, 1969). Since that time, all US zoning controls must be grounded in "health, safety, and welfare" justifications. Affordable housing has, for over a decade, been accepted as a valid rationale for decisions. Ergo landowners must sometimes accept less than optimal "highest and best use" value for their lands, even to the point of paying development taxes for the privilege of developing their land.

216   The Progressive Era debates on inequality and taxes were long and strident. More than a book would be needed to convey the rancor of the time on a tax we now take for granted. An income tax, or a national land tax for that matter, could not be imposed until a constitutional amendment was passed, the 16th, ultimately passed in 1909. At first it was steeply progressive, levied almost entirely on the rich. Not so today.

217   (Kautz, 2002) Barbara Kautz provides an excellent and detailed history here. California, because the housing crisis hit there first, has the deepest pool of policy responses and consequent court challenges to same.

218   (Thaden, 2017)

Figure 6-2. Santa Monica has been much more successful in supplying affordable housing than other California cities. Trends in total, market-rate and affordable housing productions in Santa Monica 2011-2017, benchmarked against San Diego, San Francisco and Los Angeles. Source: City of Santa Monica, San Diego, San Francisco and Los Angeles data, December 2018. (Nazu, 2020)

The most prevalent type of inclusionary housing policy was mandatory policies applying to all types of residential development, followed by voluntary policies on residential development. The options for developers for fulfilling their contribution to affordable housing under the inclusionary housing policies were either to build on site, while the second-most prevalent option was paying an in-lieu fee. In-lieu fees are often set lower than the cost of producing an affordable unit in an area where the new development is located, a process that works against income mixing in a single project.

Depending on the jurisdiction, anywhere from 6 to 20 percent of the newly developed units were required to be affordable. The proportion of affordable housing that is required largely depends upon the economic feasibility of an inclusionary housing policy and local political will. This study found that at least 90 percent of programs had affordability requirements that lasted for 30 years or longer.[219]

A study of the inclusionary housing (IH) program in Santa Monica shows how land value capture (siphoning off land Rents) to incentivize IH can lead to a relatable number of affordable units to market-rate units. These numbers, as shown in illustration 6-2, are stagnant in places like LA and San Diego where dramatically increased land Rent has apparently largely gone to land speculators. [220]

Cash or housing in lieu of cash exactions

The in-lieu-fee approach allows developers to contribute cash to the jurisdiction, its housing trust fund, or sometimes a designated nonprofit organization instead of building affordable units. The fee is pegged to the construction cost for a developer to add one market-rate unit to a proposed development. In general, the fee does not include land Rent cost, which is a major weakness of most cash-in-lieu payments.

Developers often choose to produce affordable units in other areas of the jurisdiction where land Rents are lower, housing characteristics are more "compatible," or existing improved lots, city-owned properties, or housing suitable for renovation are available. Some inclusionary programs provide incentives, such as density bonuses and public subsidies, to encourage production or improvement of affordable housing that spurs neighborhood revitalization. In addition, city-owned sites may be involved. The programs may require that locations of off-site development be near the proposed market-rate developments.[221]

Most studies suggest that in-lieu fees are typically set far lower than the cost of producing an affordable unit in an area where the new development is located. This reticence is yet another instance where a lack of focus on land Rent, and a political reticence to explicitly embrace the goal of driving down the cost of urban land, has limited the value of these taxing tools. [222]

The larger point to draw here is that legal tools exist to divert land Rent increases into affordable housing options, but that municipalities

---

219   (Ibid.)
220   (Nazu, 2020)
221   (Porter, 2009)
222   (Thaden, 2017)

are currently reluctant to use these tools to drive down land Rents. This may be, as this volume contends, because land speculators exert disproportionate influence on local officials and have deep enough pockets for expensive court challenges.

The following table shows a comparison of the different U.S. cities that have adopted linkage/impact fees :

Location	Year started	Population	Charged on	Amount
Boston, MA	1987	673,184	Commercial developments over 100,000 sq. feet	$10.01 per sq. ft. after the first 100,000 sq. ft. $8.34 for housing & $1.67 for job training
Denver, Colorado	2017	693,060	All new developments	Muti-unit : $1.55, Sin
Winter Park, FL	1990	30,208	Commercial & Residential	$0.50/ sq. ft.
Jupiter, FL	2015		Commercial & Industrial > 2000 sq ft.	$1/ sq. ft. after 2000 sq. ft.
Arlington County, VA	2006	230,000	Commercial only	$1.77/ sq. ft. (increase subject to CPI annually)
Seattle, WA	2014	744,955	commercial and multi-family residential	$5 - $22 per sq. ft.
Boston, MA		694,583	Commercial developments over 100,000 sq. feet	$9.03 per sq. ft. for housing
Boulder, CO	2015	107,353	New market-rate developments	$30/ sq. ft (second highest in US)
San Jose, CA	2015	1.03 million	New market-rate developments	$17.00 per sq. ft.
Palo Alto		66,666	Large commercial and industrial	$19.31/sq. ft.
San Bruno	2016	43,047	- Net new residential floor area for apartments and condos - Single-family detached homes - Retail, restaurants, and services, - Hotels, offices and medical offices	- $25 per sq. of net new residential floor area - $27 per sq. ft. - $6.25 per sq. ft. of net new gross floor area - $12.50 per sq. ft.
Cambridge, MA	2010	118,977	New, non-residential developments of more than 30,000 sq. feet of gross floor area	$20.10 linkage fee per sq. ft. of gross floor area
San Diego	1990	1.426 million	new market-rate developments non-residential	$99 per 1,000 sq. ft.

Chapter 7

A modern tax on Rent: city-wide zoning approaches

Introduction

L and use zoning has been used for more than a century and is deeply supported by US case law. However, only recently has zoning been clearly understood as a means of influencing land Rent for social purpose. Two basic approaches are now being applied. The first involves a retooling of a city's basic residential area zoning codes to

Figure 7-1. Portland, Oregon. Mt. Hood in distance. Image: Google Maps.

incentivize the production of affordable units. Portland, Oregon has chosen this path. The second involves the imposition of an "overlay district" over an entire city (which does not replace existing city-wide zoning, but rather provides an alternative approval path in return for affordable housing). Cambridge, Massachusetts has chosen this path. Each model is discussed in turn below.

The City of Portland, Oregon: Adding supply and affordable units city wide

In the summer of 2020, Portland City Council voted 3-1 in favor of its "Residential Infill Proposal." [223] This, after four years of debate. The new zoning ordinance[224] brings a raft of changes to city residential zones, including limiting new single-family homes to 2,500 square feet (down from 6,500 square feet), encouraging multiple units on most lots and slashing requirements for off-street parking.

But the biggest boost to affordability will come from a provision allowing up to six dwelling units on all residentially zoned lots in the city — including the more than 50 percent of the city zoned "single-family" – in return for three affordable units." [225]

To be allowed to build the maximum six units, developers will have to ensure three of the units are made permanently affordable to average wage earners. The measure offers a pathway to achieving permanent affordability in every Portland neighborhood – at no cost to the taxpayer. The city's stated goals are to "provide opportunities for a wider variety of housing options and to reduce the cost of a single unit by roughly half the cost of a single new house."

Portland chose a more aggressive shift than Minneapolis, Minnesota which received much attention for its own city wide rezoning.[226] In Minneapolis, every single-family zone was changed to allow up to three units. However, success in providing more affordable housing has been limited.[227] The problem was twofold. First, the city did not marry the change with allowing additional density on each lot. Second, the city did not require some or all units to be permanently affordable. With no increase in allowable mass, the ordinance failed to produce additional density,

223   (Portland, 2020)
224   (Portland, City of 2020)
225   "Single family" in quotes because Portland already allows a second dwelling — or "accessory units" in areas with single-family zoning
226   (M. a. Thompson, 2019)
227   (Fink, 2019)

meaning that multiple-dwelling units could not out-compete the market for an equally sized single-family home. As well, the entire premise was that if you simply authorized a flood of potential new housing units, the market would deliver affordability gains. As discussed previously, it can't. The natural function of an area's housing market ensures that a square foot of housing in a three-unit project will not cost significantly less than a square foot in a single-family home located on the same parcel.

Portland planners, with an eye toward Minneapolis, realized that just adding allowable units without adding new density would limit the market uptake. They also realized that adding density without requiring affordability leads to land price inflation and no net gain in affordability. In the end, you just get bigger buildings with no decrease in the per-square-foot price of the units. Portland chose a more effective approach.

Builders that agree to make half of new units in formerly single-family zoned neighborhoods permanently affordable will get a substantial density bonus,[228] and utilization to build six rather than four units (provided that two of them are permanently affordable). Portland has set a strict definition of affordability. The two affordable units in six-unit buildings must be affordable for families with 60 per cent or less of the city's median income.

Also crucial: cutting the allowable size of new single-family homes on subject parcels by over 60 percent acts as a disincentive for single-family home construction and a politically palatable way to lower land Rents city wide.

It took four years' worth of meetings and 38,000 individual mailings to mitigate fears and incorporate important neighborhood residents' views into the final plan.

The ordinance requires new buildings to respect a neighborhood's character (often a difficult concern to satisfy, and even harder to define) by not overshadowing neighbors.

Importantly, the city eliminated on-site parking requirements for affordable units, freeing up space for gardens and new structures. Parking is always a contentious issue, and not everyone in the city agreed with this change. But in the end, councilors understood that affordability objectives could not be met if much of a redeveloped parcel was consumed for car storage. Also critical, the city will require the preservation of

---

228   Typically this is achieved by transferring ownership of strata-titled units to non-profit housing corporations or by being developed and managed by non-profits. Non-profit housing providers played a significant role in developing the Portland ordinance.

character homes as part of any plans.

Portland City Councilor Chloe Eudaly, a tenants' rights activist, said social and racial justice issues drove the initiative:

> *"For over 100 years, exclusionary zoning laws have kept certain types of housing, and therefore certain classes and races of people, out of single-family neighborhoods. Simple upzoning will not rem‐ edy past harms or guarantee more affordable housing and diverse neighborhoods. That is why I've worked so hard to ensure that we included incentives for affordable housing, commit to developing and implementing anti-displacement measures, and encourage the preservation of existing housing,"* [229]

A low-rise scale is kept in existing neighborhoods, with a range of housing options that promote housing affordability and compatible housing forms. Importantly, no land assembly is required to densify. And the approvals process is significantly simplified.

This ordinance creates new opportunities for existing homeowners to add density on their properties to better accommodate aging in place and to free up equity when they need it without selling and moving away. The strategy also allows for separate housing units for grown-up children who can't afford to buy back into the neighborhoods where they grew up.

There are legitimate criticisms of the changes. The requirement for af‐ fordability only kicks in when six units are planned. If developers choose, they can build four units, and those four can be sold or rented at mar‐ ket-rates. There is a fear most projects may just add expensive units, dis‐ placing families and realizing no social benefits. And the bylaw does not specify the size of the affordable units, so there is an incentive to make them very small and unsuitable for families.

These concerns illuminate the necessity of carefully calibrating the re‐ quirements of such an ordinance. Not mentioned since Chapter two, but still relevant: American wage rates have not kept up with home costs. In jobs-rich coastal cities this gap is yawing. The higher the gap the harder it is to make projects work without demanding rents too high for medi‐ an-income earners. The wider the gap between current wages and current land prices the fewer will be the social benefits that can be demanded and still have projects pencil out without subsidy.

---

229   (KATU, 2020)

Given current land and wage rates in Portland, one fears that they could have insisted that at least 50 percent of the floor space of six-unit projects be affordable and require at least one affordable unit in the new fourplexes. In the end, the Portland ordinance seems to reveal a mixture of a belief in the power of new supply to lower prices by adding more market units (as in the Minneapolis model), and a recognition that land Rent is the problem and must be stopped in its tracks. This may be an uncomfortable compromise between two opposed interpretations of the problem.

Nevertheless, the Portland model is a clear breakthrough that could be adapted immediately in other US cities.

The City of Cambridge affordable housing overlay district. Best in class

Citizens and policy makers in Cambridge, Massachusetts have discovered a powerful new way to stem the seemingly inexorable rise in city land Rents, by directing all new density gains away from speculator profits toward social purpose. They have imposed an ordinance that authorizes a doubling of allowable density city wide in return for building only

Figure 7-2. Cambridge Massachusetts foreground. Boston Massachusetts rear ground. Image: City of Cambridge.

permanently affordable housing units. They achieved this by adopting a new zoning bylaw in the fall of 2020 named the "Affordable Housing Overlay District" (AHO). It is called an overlay district because it does not change the base zoning of a parcel, but "overlays" parcels and districts with a second set of more generous rules, should developers choose to conform to them.

The Cambridge AHO is less subject to court challenges than some of the strategies discussed in Chapter six because it does not "exact" concessions as a condition of project approval. Unlike landowners subject to blanket requirements for inclusive zoning or housing impact fees, landowners in AHO zones remain perfectly free to adhere to existing zoning should they wish. However, if owners/developers opt to conform to the affordability constraints of the overlay district they can add more density than the underlying zoning allows. Why does this matter? By not changing the underlying zoning, you do not send a signal to the land markets that there may be speculative land value increases in store. Ideally, land prices stay stable.

Non-profit housing development corporations are especially favored by this model as they are institutionally equipped to both build and manage this kind of housing.

The Cambridge AHO[230] covers the entirety of the city, not just one district. It authorizes an increase in allowable density up to a floor-surface ratio of 2 (FSR 2). This is more than double the typical density of parcels in this city of largely detached wood-frame homes. In order to qualify for a permit under the standards set forth in the ordinance, proponents must agree that 100 percent of new or refurbished units will be permanently affordable. Affordability thresholds are set in the ordinance so that rent is no more than 30 percent of a resident's gross income. 80 percent of the units would be available to households at 30 to 80 percent of the area's median income, with some of that number going to residents with housing vouchers, and 20 percent of units available at 80 to 100 percent of the area's median income. These numbers may seem arcane to those not familiar with this parlance, but they are crucial. In jobs-rich coastal cities like Cambridge (Cambridge MA is functionally a part Boston proper), and as explained in previous Chapters, average wages are far too low relative to the cost of housing. Pegging housing costs at 30 percent of median wages rectifies this disparity. If produced in significant

---

230   (City of Cambridge, 2020)

numbers throughout the city, it is conceivable that a reasonable mix of incomes may be achieved in a city that, like many others of its kind, is rapidly becoming a community solely for the rich (or in technical terms, only for the upper quintile of income earners).

What does all this planner speak have to do with the subject of land Rents? It's worth illustrating why this is relevant, using Cambridge as the example.

If you simply increase allowable density without requiring affordability, here is what happens: Imagine a 4,000 square foot parcel with an allowable floor/surface ratio of 1 (FSR 1) selling for $2 million prior to rezoning. After the allowable density is doubled (FSR 2), the potential redevelopment value increases in kind, forcing a near doubling in the value of the land.

Why?

When the city authorizes new density, the land price goes up but the price per buildable square foot stays roughly the same. You get more efficient use of the land but no substantial decrease in the cost per square foot of new housing. This is because the housing market does not price housing in the cost of a square foot of dirt, but rather in the eventual sale price of a square foot of finished interior space.

Lets assume the average single family zoned home parcel is worth 2 million dollars, and that most of that value is land value (this is the case in Cambridge). However, redevelopment sites are priced not per square foot of dirt but by how much you are allowed through zoning to build on it.

In hot markets, the price per square foot of usable interior space can be $1,000 or more. At that price, a developer can afford to pay roughly $500 per "buildable" square foot, because after accounting for construction costs ($250 per sq ft.), profits and fees ($250 per sq. ft.), she knows she can afford the $500 per square foot "buildable," or roughly $4 million for the land. Thus, the home purchaser (or renter) receives no cost benefit (per square foot) for this added density. All of that new value goes to the landowner – to Rent.

As has been mentioned many times in this volume, what has just been just stated as fact is a matter of fierce and likely never-ending debate. Proponents of adding density, without insisting on affordability benefits, claim that land and unit prices will drop as cities "add supply," invoking the so-called laws of supply and demand to make their case. They insist that this is the way to lower prices and that restrictive zoning, which restricts supply, is the problem. The evidence does not support their claim. Rather, the evidence shows that increases in allowable density (particularly in the jobs-rich coastal cities where Rent levels are inflating rapidly) merely increase land price, i.e. increase the level of Rent, with the only benefit going to land speculators.

Now on the other hand, if the city only authorizes density increases if all units are affordable, the numbers for the project change considerably. We can work it backward from the incomes of the people we want to house. To make the math easy, our target family makes $66,000 per year (roughly median US household income). Thus, they can pay 30 percent of their gross income, or $20,000 yearly for the rent or mortgage of their home. This amount will finance a $450,000, 20 year mortgage at 3 percent interest. Such a person might afford a 600 square foot unit, meaning the purchase price per square foot would be roughly $750. Working again backwards to the "residual" value for the land, we have $250 per square foot for construction and $250 per square foot for profit and other costs. That leaves $250 per square foot "buildable" to pay for the land. Given that the total allowable square foot of built space (on this 4,000 square foot lot – at the new FSR of 2) is 8,000 square foot, the builder can afford to pay $2 million for the land.

That's the "residual" price for the land, the same as its price under current zoning. Cost per square foot sale price goes from $1,000 down to $750 with all of that price drop attributable to lower land cost, i.e. lower Rent. All other costs are the same. The second, and especially important way to think about this process is that the parcel can still be marketed at its existing high value as a single-family home. No one loses. But the developer of affordable housing can now compete for the same parcel on equal footing with the wealthy single-family home purchaser.

As you can perhaps understand, this math becomes more and more important as land prices climb. In places like Cambridge, land prices can be higher than the ones used in this demonstration, and the need for this approach that much greater.

There are two more important points. The Cambridge ordinance is structured to insist that units be affordable forever. This means that land Rent, rather than being tied to the global appetite for investment assets, as is now the case, is forevermore tied to local wage rates. As long as the policy holds, the ultimate cost of land will be tied to 30 percent of prevailing wages. If a substantial percentage of the city eventually is redeveloped in this way, the city's land base is protected from excessive Rent in perpetuity.

A second and related point: regulating Rent in this way means that the local economy will be more and more tied to the productive value of its internal labor pool and active capital without the cash value of those activities being absorbed as Rent. This point makes it clear that pegging land Rents to wages has positive knock-on effects on the local economy as well.

Chapter 8

Summation

A calculation of total annual American urban land value increase

I t is worth reminding citizens and policy makers how massive are the capital flows coursing through the urban lands of American cities. Absent a deep appreciation for this flow, it is difficult to grasp its relevance. The following figures attempt to place these capital flows in their proper perspective.

The value of all urban land in every US metropolitan area combined is in the range of \$30 – \$35 trillion.[231] To give the reader some sense of scale, the annual GDP of the USA is around \$20 trillion.[232] Since 2010, the value of America's housing has grown by 50 percent, or roughly \$15 trillion.[233] Yearly increases in American GDP were in the range of \$1 trillion meaning that the annual increase in urban land value substantially exceeded total annual GDP growth. Of this \$1.5-trillion annual increase in urban land value, over 80 percent was attributable to the increase in the value of existing homes.[234] This \$1.2-trillion annual value increase can be safely ascribed to the increase in land value, since

---

231   Estimates of urban land value range broadly due to incompatible and incomplete data. The best estimate is from (Albouy, 2017) and includes 324 designated urban metropolitan areas, but excludes non-metropolitan urban areas. A more accessible summary article using the same data is by Richard Florida (R. Florida, 2017). These values were from the years between 2005 and 2010 and thus include the Great Recession. Urban land prices have generally increased by over 50 percent on average since then.
232   (Bureau of Economic Analysis, Department of Commerce, 2020)
233   (Manhertz, 2020)
234   (Manhertz, Recovery Riches: The U.S. Housing Market Gained \$11 Trillion in Value in the 2010s 2020)

buildings (according to our tax codes) actually depreciate in value every year, much like cars.

The number above, $30-plus-trillion for all metropolitan lands in the country, is likely low when considered against the fact that the value of just the privately owned land of Manhattan, an island just 23 square miles in area, is approximately $2 trillion.[235] The value of Manhattan's private lands has increased by 3,000 percent since 1995 (or when adjusted for inflation, by 2,000 percent). The crash of 2008 barely slowed this increase. While Manhattan is certainly an extreme example, it is not uncharacteristic. Metropolitan-area urban and suburban land in America's so-called "super cities," – New York, Los Angeles, San Francisco, Washington, D.C., and Chicago – are burdened with land prices per acre that average in the low millions per acre.[236]

This value increase for urban land does not add one bit to the nation's production of goods and services. In other words, it's not part of the "real" economy. It is simply, and frighteningly, a measure of the annual increase in land Rent – money passively filling the pockets of urban landowners and speculators.

Capturing only the annual increase in the value of already developed urban lands would generate over $900 billion annually, or enough to build between 4 and 8 million homes each year. Four to eight million is actually a large understatement, because the monthly payments supplied by residents of these new units, pegged to 30 percent of average American incomes, would amortize the cost of double or triple this number – up to 24 million homes. These massive numbers are provided here to give the reader a sense of just how much money is passing through various hands at the municipal level in the US, and how much this flow is increasing social and economic inequality.

These gains are flowing largely to real-estate investors and to older White upper-middle-class Americans – Americans who are already well off and getting richer through passively acquired gains. If planning and urban development controls were adjusted to capture even a portion of this land value gain, we could strategically address, and substantially alleviate, the racial, economic, intergenerational, and epidemiological geographic inequities outlined in Chapter 1 and 2 – and the only losers would be the land speculators.

---

235   (Barr, 2018)
236   (R. Florida, 2017)

Wielding policy tools to increase wellbeing and social justice

Policy solutions already exist that could dramatically reverse the current harmful trends toward ever-greater geographic inequality caused by ever-higher land Rent. This is no small thing. In Chapters one and two, facts were provided that proved the connection between geographic inequality and communicable disease, racial injustice, and economic inequality. Accepting that, it is also clear that policies are available to redress these serious dangers. Furthermore, development policies that limit owner land Rents have passed constitutional barriers. Policy makers are free to use taxing and planning policies to reverse inequitable and dangerous land price trends – to reverse the explosion of land Rent. In fact, these policies are already being used in many parts of the country.

However the crucial issue, that of the destructive consequence of Rent, is rarely given voice in these policy debates. If it is clear that public bodies must favor the health, safety and welfare of citizens when in conflict with maximizing landowner Rents, then actions to reduce or at least stabilize land Rent seems obligatory. The easiest way to slow or stop the ever-accelerating rise in urban land Rents is to use zoning and development tax tools to this end. The strategies outlined in previous Chapters do slow or reverse the rise in urban land Rents, while they simultaneously increase our national stock of non-market housing. It will take time, but with a more aggressive policy the US may, in time, approach Vienna levels of permanently affordable housing, available to every income class, and at no cost to the taxpayer. The funding would all come from Rent.

Author's end note

For four decades, urbanists, including this author, have lobbied hard for walkable mixed-use, mixed-income, color-blind, medium-density developments. We have had much success in this combined effort. While certainly not yet the norm in our American urban landscapes, the goals of this movement have been largely incorporated into the planning ambitions of most metropolitan municipalities.

But the hard truth is our efforts have been ineffective. During these same four decades, our communities have become ever-more segregated by race and class, and the goal of an affordable home, in a suitable neighborhood, within which to raise a family, or to simply live without stress, has slipped further and further away. Now at least half of all Americans are experiencing housing stress and blocked access to appropriate housing.

Into this uncomfortable reality now bursts a pandemic. The pandemic underlines a problem too long ignored: the way our metropolitan landscapes are organized is killing the very people who least deserve it.

Why is this so? Is there evil intent behind our planning and development decisions? This author likes to think not. It's not that we are trying to build social and health dysfunctions into our planning decisions. It is rather that we have for far too long ignored the real problem: land Rent. All of our best efforts have only directed gains to land speculators and to those upper-middle-class (largely White) families lucky enough to own a plot of land.

Unequal access to land was softened and disguised during the three decades following WWII. But in recent decades, particularly the last two and particularly in our jobs-rich coastal cities, the damage inflicted by out-of-control land price is unconscionable. As Henry George correctly pointed out 130 years ago, progress, far from being an unreserved good thing, actually produces poverty. And it's the monopoly cancer of land

Rent that is the cause. As a city makes progress, adding jobs and skilled labor, all of that creative energy gets inexorably vacuumed into land price, up to and beyond the point where lowest-wage workers live a precarious existence where one life tragedy puts them on the street: poverty.

This urbanist has reluctantly concluded that there is no way for the "free market" to overcome this pathology, no matter how much new density we approve. Adding density only enriches the land speculator and adds fuel to the fires of unbridled land Rent. The solution must be, as Vienna discovered so long ago, to harness land Rent for social purpose. In doing so, you create security for wage earners (labor) and opportunity for entrepreneurs (capital).

What we have forgotten, and the thing that Henry George tried valiantly to demonstrate during his too-short life, was that labor and capital are not opposed. They are on the same side. Their common enemy is land Rent. This polemic may seem harsh, but the solutions are surprisingly simple (at least to the mind of this author). We already possess the policy tools to stop land rent inflation, and even reverse it, through intelligent use of the already constitutionally approved and no-cost tools of zoning and development controls.

It's almost too boring to be true – but it is. The slightly arcane rules and regulations of everyday planning practice, at the local level, are the Archimedes lever we need. Would that we can collectively understand this and gather the political will to use them effectively. Our kids and grandkids are depending on us.

Bibliography

Ahlfeldt, Gabriel M. and Pietrostefani, Elizabetta. 2017. The Economic Effects of density: A synthesis. Munich Society for the Promotion of Economic Research - CESifo.

Albouy, David and Ehrlich, Gabriel. 2017. "Metropolitan Land Values1." University of Illinois, Campaign-Urbana. https://experts.illinois.edu/en/publications/metropolitan-land-values

Arrington, Benjamin. 2012. Free homes for free men: A political history of the homestead act. Topeka: Digital Commons University of Kansas.

Azar, Alex, interview by Jake Tapper. 2020. Azar lays part of blame for COVID-19 death toll on state of Americans' health CNN. May 17. https://www.cnn.com/2020/05/17/politics/us-health-conditions-coronavirus-alex-azar-cnntv/index.html

Babcock, Richard and Bosselman, Fred. 1973. Exclusionary Zoning in the 1970s. New York: Praeger

Baker, Marissa. 2020. Non-relocatable Occupations at Increased Risk During Pandemics. April 18. https://ajph.aphapublications.org/doi/full/10.2105/AJPH.2020.305738

Balk, Kristen and Fry, Richard. 2019. Millennial life: How young adulthood today compares with prior generations. February 14. https://www.pewsocialtrends.org/essay/Millennial-life-how-young-adulthood-today-compares-with-prior-generations/

Barber, William J. and Dolan, Karen. 2018. "Trump's war on the poor has just begun." The Washington Post, July 18. https://www.washingtonpost.com/opinions/trumps-war-on-the-poor-has-just-begun/2018/07/18/ae0a1b3c-8abc-11e8-85ae-511bc1146b0b_story.html

Barr, Jason and .Smith, Fred et al. 2018. "What's Manhattan worth? A land values index from 1950 to 2014." Regional Science and Urban

Economics 70.

Bauman, John F., and Roger, eds. Biles. 2000. From Tenements to the Taylor Homes: In Search of an Urban Housing Policy in Twentieth century America. Pennsylvania State University Press.

Beckett, Andy. 201. "The right to buy: the housing crisis that Thatcher built." The Guardian, August 26: 5.

Been, Vicki. 2005. "Impact Fees and Housing Affordability." Cityscape: A Journal of Policy Development and Research 8 (1). https://www.huduser.gov/periodicals/cityscpe/vol8num1/ch4.pdf

Bell, Michael E. and Bowman, John H. 2006. Methods of Valuing Land for Real Property Taxation:. Cambridge, Ma.: Lincoln Institute of Land Policy. https://www.lincolninst.edu/sites/default/files/pubfiles/1120_Bowman_complete_web.pdf

Bell, Michael. 2002. Methods of Valuing Land for Real Property Taxation:. Lincoln Institute of Land Policy. https://www.lincolninst.edu/sites/default/files/pubfiles/1120_Bowman_complete_web.pdf

Berg, Steve. 2014. "Housing programs concentrate poverty in a few metro locations, report finds." MinnPost, July 2. https://www.minnpost.com/politics-policy/2014/02/housing-programs-concentrate-poverty-few-metro-locations-report-finds/

Bloom, Nicholas Dagen. 2016. Affordable Housing in New York: The People, Places, and Policies That Transformed a City. Princeton, New Jersey: Princeton University Press.

Boarderless Charity, Inc. 2017. Public Housing in the United States: Where It is Today. December 15. https://medium.com/@TheCharity/public-housing-in-the-united-states-where-it-is-today-761826f6a43

Boerne, Dean. 2020. After Supreme Court Denial, What's Next For NIMBYs And Inclusionary Zoning? January 7. https://www.bisnow.com/national/news/affordable-housing/whats-next-for-inclusionary-zoning-102410

Brooks, David. 2020. "How Moderates Failed Black America." New York Times, June 18. https://www.nytimes.com/2020/06/18/opinion/black-america-education.html?action=click&block=associated_collection_recirc&impression_id=769041678&index=0&pgtype=Article&region=footer

Bryan, William Jennings. 1897. "One of the Foremost thinkers of the world." New York Times, October 30. https://timesmachine.nytimes.com/ timesmachine/1897/10/30/105956689.pdf

Bullard, Robert D. 1991. The Wrong Complexion for Protection: How the Government Response to Disaster Endangers African American Communities. New York: New York University Press.

Bureau of Economic Analysis, Department of Commerce. 2020. Gross Domestic Product, Fourth Quarter and Year 2019 (Advance Estimate). January . https://www.bea.gov/news/2020/gross-domestic-product-fourth-quarter-and-year-2019-advance-estimate

Burnett, Kimberly et. al. 2008. Research on State and Local Means of Increasing Affordable Housing. National Association of Home Builders . https://www.nahb.org/-/media/NAHB/nahb-community/ docs/research-on-state-and-local-means-of-increasing-affordable-housing-2008.pdf

Canada, Statistics. 2020. Building construction price indexes, percentage change, quarterly. July 8. https://www150.statcan.gc.ca/t1/tbl1/en/ tv.action?pid=1810013502

Caro, Robert. 1974. The power broker: Robert Moses and the fall of New York. New York: Knopf.

Casselman, Ben. 2015. The Tax Deductions Economists Hate. April 3. https:// fivethirtyeight.com/features/the-tax-deductions-economists-hate/

Center on Budget and Policy Priorities. 2019. Federal Rental Assistance Fact Sheets. December 10. https://www.cbpp.org/research/housing/ federal-rental-assistance-fact-sheets#US

Chicago : Council of Planning Librarians,. 1987. Pruitt-Igoe: an annotated bibliography. Chicago: Council of Planning Librarians.

City of Cambridge. 2020. "Affordable Housing Overlay Ordinance." City of Cambridge MA., June 10. https://www.cambridgema. gov/-/media/Files/CDD/ZoningDevel/Amendments/2020/ affordablehousingoverlay2020refiled/zngamend_aho_ petition_20200610.pdf.

City of Portland. 2019. "ACCESSORY DWELLING UNITS." Ordinance. https://www.portland.gov/sites/default/files/2020-09/accessory-dwelling-units_final_signed_031519.pdf

Condon, Patrick. 2010. Seven rules for sustainable communities. Washington, D.C. : Island Press.

—. 2018. "How Vienna Cracked the Case of Housing Affordability." The Tyee, June 6. https://thetyee.ca/Solutions/2018/06/06/Vienna-Housing-Affordability-Case-Cracked/

Corbusier, Le. 1967. The radiant city : elements of a doctrine of urbanism to be used as the basis of our machine-age civilization / Le Corbusier; translated from the French by Pamela Knight, Eleanor Levieux, Derek Coltman. London: Faber, 1967.

Cox, Lawanda. 1958. "The Promise of Land for the Freedmen." The Mississippi Valley Historical Review (Oxford University Press on behalf of Organization of American Historians) Vol. 45, No. 3 (No. 3).

Crain, Caleb. 2019. "State of the Unions." The New Yorker, August 19. https://www.newyorker.com/magazine/2019/08/26/state-of-the-unions

Dadkhah, Springer, Berlin, Heidelberg. 2009. The Reagan-Thatcher Revolution: The Age of Hayek and Schumpeter. Berlin: Springer.

Daniel, Pete. 1979. "The Metamorphosis of Slavery, 1865-1900." The Journal of American History (Oxford University Press on behalf of Organization of American Historians) 66 (1).

Data USA. 2020. https://datausa.io/profile/geo/fitchburg-ma

Davidson, Nial. 2011. Historical Materialism 19 (4).

De Mille, Agnes George. 1993. Who was Henry George. Accessed July 1, 2020. https://web.archive.org/web/20060212232234/http://www.henrygeorgefoundation.us/who

Demographia. 2000. International Urbanized Areas Ranked:. July 29. http://www.demographia.com/db-intlua-popratior.htm

Dewey, John. 1928. Significant Paragraphs from Henry George's Progress and Poverty. New York: Robert Schalkenbach Foundation.

Dickens, Charles. 1842. American Notes. Chapman & Hall.

dollars.com. n.d. Historical pricing for Cars since 1953. https://www.in2013dollars.com/New-cars/price-inflation

Dougherty, Connor. 2020. "12 People in a 3-Bedroom House, Then the Virus

Entered the Equation." New York Times, August 1. https://www.nytimes.com/2020/08/01/business/economy/housing-overcrowding-coronavirus.html

Douglas, Erin. 2020. "Wage and salary growth in Houston among slowest lowest in U.S." Houston Chronicle, Feb 7. https://www.houstonchronicle.com/business/bizfeed/article/Wage-and-salary-growth-in-Houston-among-slowest-15035759.php#:~:text=Total%20compensation%2C%20too%2C%20which%20includes,about%202.6%20%%20a%20year

Duffin, Erin. 2020. U.S. population share by generation 2019. July 20. https://www.statista.com/statistics/296974/us-population-share-by-generation/

Duncan, Greg J. , Murname, Richard. 2011. Whither Opportunity. New York City: Sage Foundation.

Editorial Board. 2019. "America's Millennial Baby Bust." Wall Street Journal, May 28. https://www.wsj.com/articles/americas-Millennial-baby-bust-11559086198

Evans, Michele, K et al. 2020. "Diagnosing and Treating Systemic Racism." The New England Journal of Medicine, June 10. https://www.nejm.org/doi/full/10.1056/NEJMe2021693

Fearn, Hannah. 2014. "If housing were seen as infrastructure there would be a lot more of it." The Guardian, January 31. https://www.theguardian.com/housing-network/editors-blog/2014/jan/31/affordable-housing-infrastructure-investment

Fidler, Derek. 2019. The cost of housing is tearing our society apart. January 9. https://www.weforum.org/agenda/2019/01/why-housing-appreciation-is-killing-housing/

Fink, Camile. 2019. Opinion: End of Single-Family Zoning Won't Solve Minneapolis' Housing Problems. Oct 8. https://www.planetizen.com/news/2019/10/106557-opinion-end-single-family-zoning-won-t-solve-minneapolis-housing-problems

Florida, Richard. 2019. "Does Upzoning Boost the Housing Supply and Lower Prices? Maybe Not." Bloomberg Citylab, January 31. https://www.bloomberg.com/news/articles/2019-01-31/zoning-reform-isn-t-a-silver-bullet-for-u-s-housing

—. 2013. "How Walkability Shapes Political Activism." Bloomberg Citylab, July 5. https://www.bloomberg.com/news/articles/2013-07-05/

how-walkability-shapes-political-activism

—. 2017. "The Staggering Value of Urban Land." Bloomberg, November 22. https://www.bloomberg.com/news/articles/2017-11-02/ america-s-urban-land-is-worth-a-staggering-amount

Fontinelle, Amy. 2019. American Debt: Mortgage Debt Reaches $8.94 Trillion in 1Q 2018. June 25. https://www.investopedia.com/personal-finance/ american-debt-mortgage-debt/

Förster, Wolfgang and Menking, William Eds. 2016. The Vienna Model: Housing for the Twenty-First century City. Berlin: Jovis.

Fox, Stephen R. 1985. "The Amateur Tradition: People and Politics" The American Conservation Movement: John Muir and His Legacy. Madison Wisconsin: University of Wisconsin.

Freddie Mac. 2019. Profile of Today's Renter and Homeowner. Freddie Mac. http://www.freddiemac.com/fmac-resources/research/pdf/Freddie_ Mac_Profile_of_Todays_Renter_and_Homeowner.pdf

Friedman, Milton. 1962. Capitalism and Freedom. Chicago: University of Chicago Press.

Fuchs, Hailey. 2020. "Trump Moves to Roll Back Obama Program Addressing Housing Discrimination." The New York Times, July 23. https://www. nytimes.com/2020/07/23/us/politics/trump-housing-discrimination-suburbs.html

Furth, Salum. 2020. Automobiles Seeded the Massive Coronavirus Epidemic in New York City. April 19. https://marketurbanism.com/2020/04/19/ automobiles-seeded-the-massive-coronavirus-epidemic-in-new-york-city/

Gaffney, Mason. 1993. Neo-classical Economics as a Stratagem against Henry George. Sydney, NSW: Macquarie University School of Economic and Financial Studies. https://masongaffney.org/publications/K1Neo-classical_Stratagem.CV.pdf

Gafney, Mason and Harrison, Fred. 1994. The corruption of economics. London: : Shepheard-Walwyn in association with Centre for Incentive Taxation.

Galbraith, John Kenneth. 1958. The Affluent Society . Boston: Houghton Mifflin.

GAO. 2000. Local Growth Issues—Federal Opportunities and Challenges. Washington DC: GAO. https://www.gao.gov/assets/240/230572.pdf

Garner, Anne. 2015. Cholera Comes to New York City. February 3. https://nyamcenterforhistory.org/2015/02/03/cholera-comes-to-new-york-city/

George, Henry. 1879. Progress and Poverty. New York: D. Appleton and Co. .

George, Henry Jr. 1900. The Life of Henry George . Poole.

Gotham, Kevin Fox. 2000. " Separate and Unequal: The Housing Act of 1968 and the Section 235 Program." Sociological Forum 15 (1).

Gov. UK. n.d. Renting social housing. https://www.ethnicity-facts-figures.service.gov.uk/housing/social-housing/renting-from-a-local-authority-or-housing-association-social-housing/latest#:~:text=data%20'shows%20that%3A-,in%202016%20to%202018%2C%2017%25%20of%20households%20(3.9%20million,Briti

Grounded Solutions. 2019. Linkage Fee Programs. https://inclusionaryhousing.org/designing-a-policy/program-structure/linkage-fee-programs/

Gutheil-Knopp-Kirchwald, Gerlinde and Kadi, Justin. 2017. "Housing policy and spatial inequality: recent insights from Vienna and Amsterdam." In Public or private goods? : Redefining Res Publica , by Unger Bridgette. Cheltenham, UK: Elgaronline Elgar Economics.

Gutman, David. 2020. "After months of pleading for social distancing, health officials support protests. Seattle Black Lives Matter warns of dangers." The Seattle Times 2020, June 5. https://www.seattletimes.com/seattle-news/health/after-months-of-pleading-for-coronavirus-social-distancing-health-officials-supportive-of-protests-black-lives-matter-calls-them-too-dangerous/

Habberman, Maggie. 2017. "Munchin's Wife Mocks Oregon Woman over Lifestyle and Wealth." New York Times, August 22.

Harris, Dr Jeffery E. 2020. "Why the subways are a prime suspect: Scientific evidence that NYC public transit spread the coronavirus." New York Daily News, April 19. https://www.nydailynews.com/opinion/ny-oped-why-the-subways-are-a-prime-culprit-20200419-kkqwbd5yx5gk7awngy4d7j4zfa-story.html

Harris, Jeffery E. 2020. "The Subways Seeded the Massive Coronavirus

Epidemic in New York City." National Bureau of Economics Research, Working Paper 27021. http://web.mit.edu/jeffrey/harris/HarrisJE_WP2_COVID19_NYC_24-Apr-2020.pdf

Harvard School of Public Health. 2020. "Coronavirus and Air Pollution." July. https://www.hsph.harvard.edu/c-change/subtopics/coronavirus-and-pollution/

Hawes, Michael. 2010. The Law of Rent – the concept. August 25. https://www.ethicaleconomics.org.uk/2010/08/the-law-of-rent-the-concept/#:~:text=The%20Law%20of%20Rent%2C%20as,'&text=Economic%20rent%20is%20a%20'surplus%2C%20not%20a%20charge

Hayek, Friedrich. 1944. The road to serfdom. Chicago: University of Chicago Press.

Hays, R. Allen. 1995. The Federal Government and Urban Housing: Ideology and Change in Public Policy. Albany N.Y. : State University of New York Press.

Henry George Foundation. 2010. Winston Churchill & Henry George. https://www.ethicaleconomics.org.uk/2010/10/winston-churchill-henry-george/

Hepburn, Cameron et al. 2020. Will COVID-19 fiscal recovery packages accelerate or retard progress on climate change? Smith School Working Paper 20-02, Oxford Review of Economic Policy. https://www.smithschool.ox.ac.uk/publications/wpapers/workingpaper20-02.pdf

Home for all San Mateo County. n.d. Housing overlay zones (HOZS). https://homeforallsmc.org/toolkits/housing-overlay-zones/

Horowitz, E. 2018. "Go a few more miles in your career." The Boston Globe, February 16. https://www.bostonglobe.com/business/2018/02/16/few-more-miles-your-career/kjz1TuspX1i02dLYS1NHjL/story.html

Hueble, Steve. 2019. Homeownership Rates in Canada Still Among Highest Globally. March 4. https://www.canadianmortgagetrends.com/2019/03/homeownership-rates-in-canada-still-among-highest-globally/#:~:text=As%20of%202016%20(the%20most,a%20homeownership%20rate%20of%2063.4%25

Jackson, Kenneth T. 1985. Crabgrass frontier: the suburbanization of the United States. New York: Oxford University Press.

Jacobs, Jane. 1961. The Death and Life of Great American Cities. New York: Random House.

Jan, Tracy. 2018. "Redlining was banned 50 years ago. It's still hurting minorities today." The Washington Post, March 28. https://www.washingtonpost.com/news/wonk/wp/2018/03/28/redlining-was-banned-50-years-ago-its-still-hurting-minorities-today/

Jones, Chuck. 2020. "Ignore GDP Plunging 33%. Pay Attention To The 9.5% Decline." Forbes, July 31. https://www.forbes.com/sites/chuckjones/2020/07/31/ignore-gdp-plunging-33-pay-attention-to-the-95-decline/#423332640c6a

Jones, Peter. 1987. "Henry George and British Labor Politics." The American Journal of Economics and Sociology Vol. 46, No. 2: 245-256. https://www-jstor-org.ezproxy.library.ubc.ca/stable/3485997

KATU. 2020. "Portland City Council passes Residential Infill Project." KATU2, August 12. https://katu.com/news/local/portland-city-council-passes-residential-infill-project

Kautz, Barbara. 2002. "In Defense of Inclusionary Zoning: Successfully Creating Affordable Housing." University of San Francisco Law Review 36. https://repository.usfca.edu/cgi/viewcontent.cgi?article=1060&context=usflawreview

Kelly, Kate. 2020. "'The Big Short 2.0': How Hedge Funds Profited Off the Pain of Malls." The New York Times, Aug. 24 24. https://www.nytimes.com/2020/08/24/business/mall-short-hedge-funds.html

Keyser Marston Associates, Inc. 2016. "Affordable housing nexus studies, City of Albany California." California nexus study. . https://alamedamgr.files.wordpress.com/2018/07/albany-affordable-housing-nexus-study-december-2016.pdf

King, Dr. Martin Luther. 2003. A Testament of Hope: The Essential Writings and Speeches. New York: Harper Collins.

Knoll, Katharina et al. 2014. "Federal Reserve Bank of Dallas, Globalization and Monetary Policy Institute Working Paper No. 208." https://www.dallasfed.org/~/media/documents/institute/wpapers/2014/0208.pdf

Krugman, Paul. 2020. The case for permanent stimulus. May 10. https://voxeu.org/article/case-permanent-stimulus

—. 2010. "The new economic geography , now middle aged." Association of

American Geographers,. http://www.princeton.edu/~pkrugman/aag.pdf

Landis, John, et. al. 2001. Pay to Play: Residential Development Fees in California Cities and Counties. Sacramento, CA: California Department of Housing and Community Development. https://www.novoco.com/sites/default/files/atoms/files/pay2play.pdf

Lee, Jennifer. 2008. "New York and the Panic of 1873." New York Times, October 4.

Leonhardt, David. 2020. "The Black-White Wage Gap Is as Big as It Was in 1950." New York Times, June 25. https://www.nytimes.com/2020/06/25/opinion/sunday/race-wage-gap.html

Lewis, Michael. 2011. The big short: inside the doomsday machine / Michael Lewis. New York: W.W. Norton

Linklater, Ando. 2002. Measuring America. New York: Penguin.

Locke, John. 1689. Two Treatises of Government. Awnsham Churchill.

Loyd, Aleyanna. 2019. U.S. housing market value climbs to $33.3 trillion in 2018. January 4. https://www.housingwire.com/articles/47847-us-housing-market-value-climbs-to-333-trillion-in-2018/#:~:text=In%20 2018%2C%20the%20total%20value,to%20new%20data%20from%20 Zillow

Luhby, Tami. 2020. "Nearly 40 percent of low-income workers lost their jobs in March." CNN, May 15. https://www.cnn.com/2020/05/14/economy/low-income-layoffs-coronavirus/index.html

Manhertz, Treh. 2020. Recovery Riches: The U.S. Housing Market Gained $11 Trillion in Value in the 2010's. June 16. https://www.zillow.com/research/us-total-housing-value-2019-26369/

—. 2020. Recovery Riches: The U.S. Housing Market Gained $11 Trillion in Value in the 2010's. January 16. https://www.zillow.com/research/us-total-housing-value-2019-26369/

Martin, Emmie. 2017. "Here's how much more expensive it is for you to go to college than it was for your parents." CNBC, November 29. https://www.cnbc.com/2017/11/29/how-much-college-tuition-has-increased-from-1988-to-2018.html#:~:text=Students%20at%20 public%20four%2Dyear,the%202017%2D2018%20school%20 year.&text=For%20the%202017%2D2018%20school%20year%2C%20 it's,%2434%2C740%2C%20a%20129%2

—. 2019. Here's how many Millennials got money from their parents to buy their homes. CNBC. March 20. https://www.cnbc.com/2019/03/11/how-many-Millennials-got-money-to-buy-homes-from-their-parents.html

Mass. Department of Public Health. 2020. COVID-19 Public Health Report. July 8. https://www.mass.gov/doc/weekly-COVID-19-public-health-report-july-8-2020/download

McDonnell, Tim. 2017. "Slum Dwellers In Africa's Biggest Megacity Are Now Living In Canoes." NPR. May 15. https://www.npr.org/sections/goatsandsoda/2017/05/15/528461093/slum-dwellers-in-africas-biggest-megacity-are-now-living-in-canoes

McGerr, Michael. 2003. A Fierce Discontent: The Rise and Fall of the Progressive Era. New York: Free Press .

McIntosh, , Kristen. 2020. Examining the Black-white wealth gap. February 27. https://www.brookings.edu/blog/up-front/2020/02/27/examining-the-black-white-wealth-gap/

Meja, Merisol, and Cha, Paulette. 2020. Overcrowded Housing and COVID-19 Risk among Essential Workers. May 12. https://www.ppic.org/blog/overcrowded-housing-and-COVID-19-risk-among-essential-workers/

Merritt, Keri Leigh. 2016. Land and the roots of African-American poverty. March 11. https://aeon.co/ideas/land-and-the-roots-of-african-american-poverty

—. 2017. Masterless men : poor whites and slavery in the antebellum South. Cambridge, England: Cambridge University Press.

Miller, George. 2000. On fairness and efficiency. Bristol, UK: The Policy Press.

Moore, Antonio. 2016. Inequality. October 18. https://inequality.org/research/black-wealth-exists/

Nareit. n.d. History of REITs & Real-estate Investing. https://www.reit.com/what-reit/history-reits

National Fair Housing Alliance. 2008. Dr. King's Dream Denied: Forty Years of Failed Federal Enforcement: 2008 Fair Housing Trends Report." National Fair Housing Alliance. April 8, 2008. National Fair Housing Alliance.

National Housing Law Project; the Poverty & Race Research Action Council; Sherwood Research Associates, and Everywhere and Now Public Housing Residents Organizing Nationally Together. 2002. "False Hope." http://www.narpac.org/ITXFALSE.HTM

Nazu, Bernard and Trillo, Claudia. 2020. "Harnessing the real-estate market for equitable affordable housing provision: insights from the city of Santa Monica, California." Housing Studies (Taylor & Francis). https://www.tandfonline.com/doi/ref/10.1080/02673037.2020.174624 4?scroll=top

Nero, Dorn. 2019. "In It's A Wonderful Life, Pottersville Actually Looks Way More Fun Than Bedford Falls." Esquire, December 24. https://www.esquire.com/entertainment/movies/a30315437/ its-a-wonderful-life-pottersville-better-than-bedford-falls/

Newman, Oscar. 1972. Defensible space : crime prevention through urban design. New York: Macmillan.

Nicholas, T and Scherbina, A. 2013. "Real-estate prices during the roaring twenties and the great depression." Real-estate Economics (Wiley).

NYTimes. 2018. "Political Bubbles and Hidden Diversity: Highlights From a Very Detailed Map of the 2016 Election." New York Times, July 25. https://www.nytimes.com/interactive/2018/07/25/upshot/precinct-map-highlights.html

Ocasio-Cortez, Alexandria. 2020. Ahead of Hearing, Ocasio-Cortez Condemns the Real-estate Industry's Request to Use Federal Bailout Funds to Enrich Shareholders. July 14. https://www.commondreams. org/newswire/2020/07/14/ahead-hearing-ocasio-cortez-condemns-real-estate-industrys-request-use-federal

Olick, Diana. 2018. Want to buy a house? How long you'll have to save depends on where you live. July 13. https://www.cnbc.com/2018/07/13/ want-to-buy-a-house-this-is-how-long-youll-have-to-save. html#:~:text=For%20the%20average%20renter%20buying,%%20 some%20financial%20experts%20recommend

Olorunnipa, Toluse. 2020. "Trump tries to win over 'Suburban Housewives' with repeal of anti-segregation housing rule." The Washington Post, July 23. https://www.washingtonpost.com/politics/trump-suburbs-biden-housing-suburban-housewives/2020/07/23/2f269980-ccf5-11ea-bc6a-6841b28d9093_story.html

Oppel, Richard A. et al. 2020. "The Fullest Look Yet at the Racial Inequity

of Coronavirus." New York Times , July 5. https://www.nytimes.com/
interactive/2020/07/05/us/coronavirus-latinos-african-americans-cdc-
data.html

Parker, Kim et. al. 2018. Demographic and economic trends in urban, suburban
and rural communities. May 22. https://www.pewsocialtrends.
org/2018/05/22/demographic-and-economic-trends-in-urban-
suburban-and-rural-communities/

Parker-Pope, Tara. 2020. "Can I Get Coronavirus From Riding an Elevator?"
The New York Times, May 13. https://www.nytimes.com/2020/05/13/
well/live/can-i-get-coronavirus-from-riding-an-elevator.html

Piketty, Thomas. 2020. Capital and Ideology. Cambridge, Ma.: Harvard
University Press.

—. 2014. Capital in the 21st century. Cambridge Mass: President and Fellows
of Harvard College.

Piketty, Thomas. 2014. Capital in the 21st century. Cambridge, Mass. :
Harvard University Press. Piketty, Thomas. 2015. Thomas Piketty
and Joseph Stiglitz on Inequality. April 8. https://www.youtube.com/
watch?time_continue=7500&v=Fg6UwAQJUVo&feature=emb_logo

Pinsker, Joe. 2020. "The New Boomerang Kids Could Change
American Views of Living at Home." The Atlantic , July
3. https://www.theatlantic.com/family/archive/2020/07/
pandemic-young-adults-living-with-parents/613723/

Porter, Douglas and Davison, Elizabeth. 2009. "Evaluation of In-Lieu Fees and
Offsite Construction as Incentives for Affordable Housing Production."
Cityscape (US Department of Housing and Urban Development) 11
(2). https://www.jstor.org/stable/i20868698

Portland, City of. 2020. "Introduction and Summary of the Residential Infill
Project (RIP) amendments." Council report, Portland, OR. https://
www.portland.gov/sites/default/files/2020-08/exhibit_a_rip_findings_
adopted1.pdf

Portland, City of. 2020. "ORDINANCE No. 190093 As Amended."
Portland, OR. https://www.portland.gov/sites/default/files/2020-08/
ordinance_190093_adopted1.pdf

Prager, Alicia. 2018. Vienna battles rising housing costs — can a new
policy fix it? November 2. https://www.euronews.com/2018/10/30/
vienna-battles-rising-housing-costs-can-a-new-policy-fix-it

Preiss, David L. 2017. California "In Lieu" Affordable Housing Fees Withstand Constitutional Challenge. October. https://www.hklaw.com/en/insights/publications/2017/10/california-in-lieu-affordable-housing-fees-withsta

Property Metrics. 2019. Residual Techniques in Real-estate Valuation. July 23. https://propertymetrics.com/blog/residual-techniques-in-real-estate-valuation/

Quealy, Kevin. 2020. "The Richest Neighborhoods Emptied Out Most as Coronavirus Hit New York City." New York Times, May 15. https://www.nytimes.com/interactive/2020/05/15/upshot/who-left-new-york-coronavirus.html

Quinn, Michael. 2001. "Sprawl as Strategy: City Planners Face the Bomb." Journal of Planning Education and Research Volume: 21 issue: 1.

Radford, Gail. 1996. Modern Housing for America: Policy Struggles in the New Deal Era. Chicago: University of Chicago Press.

Reiss, Veronica R. 2017. Viennese planning culture : understanding change and continuity through the Hauptbahnhof. Masters thesis. Vancouver: University of British Columbia School of Community and Regional Planning.

Reuters. 2019. "Berlin spends nearly €1 billion buying back apartments." Deutsche Welle, August 27. https://www.dw.com/en/berlin-spends-nearly-1-billion-buying-back-apartments/a-50617775

Ricardo, David. 1817. On the Principles of Political Economy and Taxation. London: John Murray.

Rice, Douglas. 2016. Chart Book: Cuts in Federal Assistance Have Exacerbated Families' Struggles to Afford Housing. April 16. https://www.cbpp.org/research/housing/chart-book-cuts-in-federal-assistance-have-exacerbated-families-struggles-to-afford

Riley, Frederick J. 2020. "Amid racial injustice and COVID-19, there's still hope America will become a better place." USA Today, July 20. https://www.usatoday.com/story/opinion/2020/07/08/why-even-amid-racial-injustice-and-COVID-19-theres-hope-america-column/5389201002/

Rothstein, Phillip. 2017. The Color of Law. New York: Liveright Publishing Corp.

Russell, Tonya. 2020. "Racism in care leads to health disparities, doctors and other experts say as they push for change." The Washington Post, July 11. https://www.washingtonpost.com/health/racism-in-care-leads-to-health-disparities-doctors-and-other-experts-say-as-they-push-for-change/2020/07/10/a1a1e40a-bb9e-11ea-80b9-40ece9a701dc_story.html

Saad, Lydia. 2020. Americans Rapidly Answering the Call to Isolate, Prepare. March 20. https://news.gallup.com/poll/297035/americans-rapidly-answering-call-isolate-prepare.aspx

Salsberg, Bob. 2018. Analysis: Blacks largely left out of high-paying jobs, government data shows. April 2. https://www.usatoday.com/story/money/2018/04/02/analysis-blacks-largely-left-out-high-paying-jobs-government-data-shows/477845002/

Sarkar, Saurav. 2018. The souls of poor folk. Washington DC: Institute for policy studies. https://ips-dc.org/wp-content/uploads/2018/04/PPC-Audit-Full-410835a.pdf#page=46

Schwartz, Gabriel and Jahn, Jaquelyn. 2020. Mapping fatal police violence across U.S. metropolitan areas: Overall rates and racial/ethnic inequities, 2013-2017. San Francisco: Plos One. https://journals.plos.org/plosone/article?id=10.1371/journal.pone.0229686

Scruggs, Gregory. 2018. "Everything we've heard about global urbanization turns out to be wrong' - researchers." Thompson Reuters Foundation. July 12. http://news.trust.org/item/20180712130016-lwnc2/

Semuels, Alana. 2015. "How Housing Policy Is Failing America's Poor." The Atlantic, June 24.

Silver, Johnathan. 2019. Here's how much Houston home prices have jumped in just 5 years. March 26. https://houston.culturemap.com/news/real-estate/03-20-19-point2-houston-home-price-increase-north-america-report/.

Simpson, Michael. 1969. VILLAGE OF EUCLID V. AMBLER REALTY CO. https://case.edu/ech/articles/v/village-euclid-v-ambler-realty-co.

Smith, Adam. 1776. The Wealth of Nations. London: W. Strahan and T. Cadell.

Smith, Nicole. n.d. Neoliberalism. https://www.britannica.com/topic/neoliberalism.

Sparkes, Sam. 2019. Poorest Cities in Massachusetts for 2020. December 24.

https://www.roadsnacks.net/poorest-places-in-massachusetts/#topTen.

Stahl, Ashley. 2020. "New Study: Millennial Women Are Delaying Having Children Due To Their Careers." Forbes, May 1. https://www.forbes.com/sites/ashleystahl/2020/05/01/new-study-Millennial-women-are-delaying-having-children-due-to-their-careers/#49439eb7276a

Stamm, Everett and Taylor LaJoie. 2020. An Overview of the Low-Income Housing Tax Credit. Washington DC: The Tax Foundation. https://files.taxfoundation.org/20200810100355/An-Overview-of-the-Low-Income-Housing-Tax-Credit.pdf

Stansbury, Anna and Summers, Larry. 2020. "Declining Worker Power and American Economic." Brookings papers on economic activity. Brookings Institute. https://www.brookings.edu/wp-content/uploads/2020/03/Stansbury-Summers-Conference-Draft.pdf

Stein, Clarence S. 1957. Toward New Towns for America, Revised Edition. MIT Press.

Stiglitz. 2020. Priorities for the COVID-19 Economy. July 1. https://www.project-syndicate.org/commentary/COVID-2020-recession-how-to-respond-by-joseph-e-stiglitz-2020-06?barrier=accesspaylog

Stolba, Stefan Lembo. 2019. Baby Boomers' Student Loan Debt Continues to Grow. July 18. https://www.experian.com/blogs/ask-experian/research/baby-boomers-and-student-loan-debt/

Summers, Graham. 2017. The Everything Bubble.

Tartar, Brent. n.d. Encyclopedia Virginia. https://www.encyclopediavirginia.org/Vagrancy_Act_of_1866

Taylor, Alan. 2011. "Occupy Wall Street Spreads Worldwide." The Atlantic, October 17. https://www.theatlantic.com/photo/2011/10/occupy-wall-street-spreads-worldwide/100171/

Thaden, Emily and Wang, Ruoniu. 2017. Inclusionary Housing in the United States: Prevalence, Impact, and Practices. Cambridge, Mass.: Lincoln Institute of Land Policy. https://www.lincolninst.edu/sites/default/files/pubfiles/thaden_wp17et1_0.pdf

The Economist. 2018. "Segregation in America." The Economist, April 4. https://www.economist.com/graphic-detail/2018/04/04/segregation-in-america

—. 2020. "Starting over again." The Economist, July 25.

The National Urban League. . 2020. The state of black America; Unmasked. New York City: The National Urban League. . http://sobadev. iamempowered.com/sites/soba.iamempowered.com/files/NUL-SOBA-2020-ES-web.pdf

The Prudential. 2019. "Gig economy impact by generation." https:// www.prudential.com/wps/wcm/connect/1b4fcef8-afc0-4c87-bc12-2ace844aecb3/Gig_Economy_Impact_by_Generation. pdf?MOD=AJPERES&CVID=mMoGiuO

The School of Cooperative Individualism. n.d. Henry George and his Principles, Albert Einstein. https://www.cooperative-individualism.org/ einstein-albert_henry-george-and-his-principles-1934.htm

Thompson, Derick. 2014. "Homeownership in America Has Collapsed—Don't Blame Millennials." The Atlantic, Oct 24. https://www.theatlantic.com/business/archive/2014/10/ homeownership-is-historically-weakdont-blame-Millennials/382010/

Thompson, M, and Saltzman, M. 2019. How Minneapolis became the first to end single-family zoning. November 19. https://www.pbs.org/newshour/show/ how-minneapolis-became-the-first-to-end-single-family-zoning

Thrush, Glen. 2020. "Trump Attacks a Suburban Housing Program. Critics See a Play for White Votes." The New York Times, July 1. https:// www.nytimes.com/2020/07/01/us/politics/trump-obama-housing-discrimination.html

Turpov, Mindy and Piper, Valerie. 2005. HOPE VI AND MIXED-FINANCE REDEVELOPMENTS:. Brookings Institute. https://web. archive.org/web/20160304060849/http://www.brookings.edu/metro/ pubs/AtlantaCaseStudy.pdf

Urban Institute. 2011. Property Taxes. https://www.urban.org/policy-centers/ cross-center-initiatives/state-and-local-finance-initiative/projects/ state-and-local-backgrounders/property-taxes.

US Bureau of Labor Statistics. 2012. Occupational employment by race and ethnicity, 2011. October 26. https://www.bls.gov/opub/ted/2012/ ted_20121026.htm

US Department of Defence. n.d. Charles E. Wilson. https://history. defense.gov/Multimedia/Biographies/Article-View/Article/571268/

charles-e-wilson/

Valentine, Ashish, interview by Ashish Valentine. 2020. 'The Wrong Complexion For Protection.' How Race Shaped America's Roadways And Cities NPR. July 5. https://www.npr.org/2020/07/05/887386869/ how-transportation-racism-shaped-america?utm_ campaign=storyshare&utm_source=twitter.com&utm_medium=social

Vincent, Joshua. 2019. Non-Glamorous Gains: The Pennsylvania Land Tax Experiment. March 6. https://www.strongtowns.org/journal/2019/3/6/ non-glamorous-gains-the-pennsylvania-land-tax-experiment

Volker, Paul Chairman. 2010. "The Report on Tax Reform Options: The President's Economic recovery advisory board." https://web.archive.org/ web/20101105201333/http://www.whitehouse.gov/sites/default/files/ microsites/PERAB_Tax_Reform_Report.pdf

Washington, Jesse. 2020. "Why did Black Lives Matter protests attract unprecedented white support?" The Undefeated, June 18. https:// theundefeated.com/features/why-did-black-lives-matter-protests-attract-unprecedented-white-support/

Wigglesworth, Robin. 2020. "How America's 1percent came to dominate stock ownership." Financial Post. , Feb 11. https://financialpost.com/ investing/how-americas-1-came-to-dominate-stock-ownership

Wikipedia. n.d. 1978 California Proposition 13. https://en.wikipedia.org/ wiki/1978_California_Proposition_13#:~:text=Proposition%2013%20 (officially%20named%20the,means%20of%20the%20initiative%20 process.&text=The%20one%20%%20(1%25),the%20districts%20 within%20the%20counties

Wikipedia. n.d. Estate tax in the United States. https://en.wikipedia.org/wiki/ Estate_tax_in_the_United_States

—. 2020. Modal share. June 14. https://en.wikipedia.org/wiki/Modal_share

Wikipedia. n.d. The Henry George Theorem. https://en.wikipedia.org/wiki/ Henry_George_theorem

Williams, Linda Faye. 2010. Constraint of Race: Legacies of White Skin Privilege in America. State College Pa. : Penn State Press.

Williamson, Elizabeth et al. 2020. OpenSAFELY: factors associated with COVID-19 death in 17 million patients. July 8. https://www.nature. com/articles/s41586-020-2521-4

Williamson, Mary Lou. 1987. Greenbelt: History of a new town, 1937-1987. Norfolk, Va: Donning Co./Publishers.

Wisconsin Historical Society. n.d. Garden Homes Historic District. https:// www.wisconsinhistory.org/Records/NationalRegister/NR1906

Wood, Gordon S. The American Revolution: A History. 2002. The American Revolution: A History. New York: Modern Library.

Wu, Katherine. 2020. "Study of 17 Million Identifies Crucial Risk Factors for Coronavirus Deaths." The New York Times, July 8. https:// www.nytimes.com/2020/07/08/health/coronavirus-risk-factors. html?searchResultPosition=1

Youn, Soo. 2019. 40 percent of Americans don't have $400 in the bank for emergency expenses: Federal Reserve. May 24. https://abcnews. go.com/US/10-americans-struggle-cover-400-emergency-expense-federal/story?id=63253846#:~:text=Almost%2040%25%20of%20 American%20adults,a%20Federal%20Reserve%20survey%20 finds.&text=However%2C%2017%25%20of%20adults%20in,of%20 their%20current%2

Zaveri, Mihir. 2020. "'I Need People to Hear My Voice': Teens Protest Racism." The New York Times, June 23. https://www.nytimes. com/2020/06/23/us/teens-protest-black-lives-matter.html

Index

Z

Manufactured by Amazon.ca
Bolton, ON

21072079R00100